D0599402

# Interactivity

## by design

# Interactivity
## by design

**Creating & Communicating
with New Media**

Adobe Press
Mountain View, CA

**Ray Kristof & Amy Satran**

Copyright © 1995 Adobe Systems Incorporated. All rights reserved. No part of this publication may be reproduced, stored in a retrieval system, or transmitted, in any form or by any means, electronic, mechanical, photocopying, recording, or otherwise, without the prior written permission of Adobe Systems Incorporated.

The information in this book is furnished for informational use only, is subject to change without notice, and should not be construed as a commitment by Adobe Systems Incorporated. Adobe Systems Incorporated assumes no responsibility for any errors or inaccuracies that may appear in this book.

The Adobe software described in this book is furnished under license and may only be used or copied in accordance with the terms of such license. Contact the software vendor directly for terms of software licenses for any software mentioned in this book not originating from Adobe Systems Incorporated.

Library of Congress Catalog No.: 95-77738

ISBN: 1-56830-221-5

10 9 8 7 6 5 4 3 2 First Printing: July 1995

Adobe, the Adobe Press logo, Acrobat, Adobe Illustrator, Adobe PageMaker, Adobe Photoshop, Aldus, and PostScript are trademarks of Adobe Systems Incorporated, which may be registered in certain jurisdictions. Other brand or product names are the trademarks or registered trademarks of their respective holders.

Printed in the United States of America.

Published simultaneously in Canada.

Published and distributed to the trade by Hayden Books, a division of Macmillan Computer Publishing. For individual, retail, corporate, educational, and government sales information, contact Macmillan Computer Publishing, 201 W. 103rd Street, Indianapolis, Indiana, 46290 USA, or call 317-581-3500.

# Contents

**What is interactivity?** ........................ 1
**Introduction** ........................ 2

**Part One: Information Design** ........................ 6
Product definition ........................ 10
Audience and environment ........................ 14
What do users want? ........................ 16
Development choices ........................ 18
Raw materials ........................ 22
Planning ........................ 24
Organization ........................ 26
The flowchart ........................ 32

**Part Two: Interaction Design** ........................ 34
Orientation ........................ 38
Image maps and metaphors ........................ 40
Navigation ........................ 42
Usability ........................ 48
Functionality ........................ 52
The storyboard ........................ 58

**Part Three: Presentation Design** ........................ 62
Digital media survival kit ........................ 66
Resolution ........................ 68
Anti-aliasing ........................ 70
Color and palettes ........................ 72
Compression is your friend ........................ 76
Laws of survival ........................ 78
Setting the style ........................ 80
How content defines style ........................ 82
Stylistic unity ........................ 84
Interface families ........................ 86
Layout ........................ 88
Layout conventions ........................ 90
Grids ........................ 92

Interface families ........................ 94
Backgrounds ........................ 96
Windows and panels ........................ 98
Buttons and other controls ........................ 100
Images ........................ 104
Text ........................ 106
Video ........................ 110
Sound ........................ 112
Animating the screen ........................ 114
Putting it all together ........................ 116
The prototype ........................ 118
Conclusion ........................ 121

**Resource guide** ........................ 122
**Credits** ........................ 126
**Index** ........................ 130

# *What is* interactivity

By definition, the things people do on computers have always been interactive. Computers and software are tools, and their purpose is to help people interact with words, numbers, and pictures. What's different today is that computers are being used for activities that never used to be considered interactive—such as reading, watching, or simply being entertained. And this means that the audience, not the designer, now controls the sequence, the pace, and most importantly, what to look at and what to ignore.

With tools for interactivity now available on every desktop, people everywhere are turning documents and presentations into interactive experiences to be viewed on the computer screen. They are discovering that adding interactivity is easy, but making interactivity really work is a whole new process—the process of creating interactivity by design.

Introduction

Research. Writing. Graphic design. Interface design. Video production. Programming. An interactive project might involve dozens of activities, and balancing these can seem impossibly complex. But it doesn't have to be, if you approach interactive design as a process.

Looking at interactive design as a process accomplishes two things:

→ It gives you a framework for visualizing how all the ideas, pictures, and other raw materials you're starting out with can be brought together into a usable interface.

→ It breaks down complex interactive projects into a set of tangible tasks and issues. This makes it possible to plan, design, and manage all the pieces of the puzzle.

Is interactive design really a process? Yes, but not a prescriptive one like painting by numbers or baking a cake. Every project has unique goals, content, and creative solutions. What's gained by seeing interactive design as a process is the ability to think about a communication project as the sum of all its parts, with a clearer sense of the underlying issues for design, usability, and production.

## One size fits all?

The process shown here can be used for all types of new media projects—delivered on-line via the Internet, on a CD-ROM disc, or by any other medium. But since different types of projects have different design issues, you'll want to apply parts of the process accordingly. For example, Part Two discusses creating a storyboard:

→ For a simple interactive document, the storyboard might show only contents and navigation.

→ For a complex multimedia CD-ROM, the storyboard might show a succession of screens including video, audio, and user interactions.

Even though the projects are different, the steps in the process leading up to the storyboards are the same.

If you're designing your first interactive project, or if you've already done one or two projects and believe there must be a better way, you'll find a design approach here that can help you make the right decisions. The level of discussion is aimed at readers who are not multimedia professionals. But the process introduced here can benefit communicators at every level.

This book is not about hardware, software, or hands-on production techniques. It's about how to identify the design and communication issues that are unique to interactive products. Unlike a product that merely has to communicate, an interactive product also has to deliver functionality and usability—it has to *work*. An interface has to provide the information access and clear guidance users need. And it should look nice, too.

To make sure these things happen, the process presented here guides you through planning, designing, and piecing together all the parts of an interface. The process can be represented as three questions, answered in the three parts of this book:

→ **What is the product?**

→ **How should it work?**

→ **How should it look?**

# The process

**Information Design**

*What is the product?*

Define the product and audience, plan the project, and organize the content into a **flowchart**

**Interaction Design**

*How should it work?*

Design the navigation, types of interaction, and controls, and map these onto a **storyboard**

**Presentation Design**

*How should it look?*

Define the style and layout of the elements in the storyboard, and produce a **prototype**

goals
message
content

design

Part One

audience
needs
environment

## Information design

means clarifying your communication
goals and arranging your ideas
into a design that serves those goals.

# Information Design

**You're here because you are about to
design an interactive product. Maybe
it's something that already exists in
another medium. Maybe it's something
new. Either way, your job begins with
information design.**

Information design is the beginning of any
interactive project—the first questions, the
process of definition. It precedes any thoughts
about what the screen will look like. But what
exactly is information design?

It's the process of clarifying your communication goals and arranging your content into a
design that serves those goals. It's selling,
teaching, storytelling, or just plain informing—
in the most effective way you can.

| If this were... | You'd start with... |
|---|---|
| a report | the outline |
| a film | the treatment |
| a painting | the charcoal sketch |

# Critical tasks of information design

→ Define goals for the product
→ Define what the audience wants to do
→ Decide how the product will reach its audience
→ Choose the authoring tool

> → Create a content inventory list
> → Create a project plan
> → Organize the content
> → Produce a content flowchart

**There is no formula for designing interactive products. But there is no interactive product that cannot benefit from clearly expressed goals, a well-defined audience, and a focused design plan. These are the building blocks of information design.**

For each stage of the interface design process—information design, interaction design, presentation design—there's a short list of critical tasks. Each of the three parts of this book begins with such a list. The tasks above make up the information design stage of the process.

Each task is a milestone in building your design. Each should help to give you a sense of direction and progress. And each should help you to come up with design solutions.

Why do so many of the critical tasks of information design look like project management? Because many things have to happen before you know what information you'll be designing. Organizing content, the activity most commonly identified with information design, is just one part of the process—the last part.

You might want to
start here.   →

## Step-by-step information design

| | | |
|---|---|---|
| **How should the content be organized?** | The term "information design" suggests you're only arranging information. But organizing content is just one part of information design. | **Organization** |
| **What content do you have the time/money/resources to create or obtain?** | Content can be organized only after you've decided what you have the resources to produce. This is the result of practical project planning. | **Planning** |
| **What technologies will you use to create and deliver the content?** | Realistic planning is possible only when the project's scope and complexity are known. These depend largely on the authoring and delivery methods you choose (Internet, CD-ROM, whatever). | **Tools** |
| **Who do you need to reach, how can you reach them, and what do they want?** | The right technology for delivering any content depends on who will use it and how. This means finding out about the needs and interests of the audience. | **Audience** |
| **What do you want this product to accomplish?** | Who you want to reach and how, in turn, depend on the product's message and purpose. Information design begins here—not by arranging content, but by defining goals. | **Goals** |

But information
design begins here.

# Let's talk about goals

# Product definition

**Goals drive your design. They define the result you seek, and give you something to measure your progress against.**

It's inevitable that to design something original and beautiful, you have to try out lots of ideas. So many, in fact, that you can lose sight of the problem you set out to solve in the first place.

The only remedy—the thing that keeps you on track—is a clearly articulated set of goals. It's the tool you use to evaluate every design decision: does this solution move the design closer to or farther from its goal?

Say you're creating an interactive reference document—maybe a catalog of publications for customers. You already have great pictures, so you design the catalog as a kind of storybook. Soon enough you have the user traveling through this storyland adventure, and your catalog has developed into a game. It's fun, but does it fulfill the product's original goal of serving as a reference?

Product definition is the first exercise of information design—the "What is the product?" stage of the process defined at the start of this book.

**Information Design**

*What is the product?*

Define the product and audience, plan the project, and organize the content into a **flowchart**

**Interaction Design**

*How should it work?*

Design the navigation, types of interaction, and controls, and map these onto a **storyboard**

**Presentation Design**

*How should it look?*

Define the style and layout of the elements in the storyboard, and produce a **prototype**

Every project begins with certain givens— the assumptions that represent your point of departure. Goals, on the other hand, represent your destination. "We're going to do an interactive publications catalog, based on our current print catalog" is a start, but it's neither an assumption nor a goal.

Nothing gets the design process off the ground like having goals defined on a piece of paper.

Begin by writing down the assumptions you're starting out with—everything you already know about what the product will be, how it will be used, and who will use it. Here are some examples of assumptions:

→ material you know has to be included, such as the content of an existing document

→ the information needs of the audience; their skills; their attitudes, interests, and preferences

It's not possible that your project has no design goals, but it is possible that you haven't expressed them yet. The goals that influence design represent what you want the product to accomplish. They don't define the product itself.

## → How do goals drive design?

| If you want users to... | Then your design might need... |
|---|---|
| **Learn and Retain** | Clarity, simplicity, directness, repetition, and reinforcement; modular breakdown of information into short presentations; testing and remediation where appropriate |
| **Have Fun** | Variety, surprises, randomness, and wit; unpredictable events that change each time the product is used |
| **Understand** | Conceptual explanations; "how it works" illustrations and video; graphs, charts, simulations |
| **Experience** | High level of interactivity; user control of actions and events; realistic sights and sounds |
| **Act or Buy** | Well defined features and benefits; a clear call to arms/options; toll-free phone number, interactive order forms, etc. |
| **Get Answers** | Reference-style organization; fast access; searchable index of contents |

The test of every design decision: does this solution move the design closer to or farther from its goals?

A goal statement, for example, would not take the form "to create an interactive publications catalog," but rather "to provide incentives for customers to purchase products on-line" or "to create an interactive publications catalog that can be updated weekly."

The latter two statements define the results you're after, and give you specific design objectives to work toward.

## Interactive Company Brochure

### Assumptions...

#### Content
brief, top-level overviews
little detail
needs to profile business units concisely

#### Audience
shareholders, potential customers, and vendors
they're busy and didn't ask for this
they have no info goals, so need to be drawn in and guided

#### Other
need to coordinate messages and styles
with ads, PR, and corporate ID

### Goals...
to project an up-to-date, techno-savvy image
to show off unique accomplishments
to engage viewers so they'll watch the whole thing
to project an image of a successful, global, socially responsible company
to motivate further inquiries

## Interactive Employee Benefits Manual

### Assumptions...

#### Content
start with existing benefits handbook

#### Audience
company internal audience only
wants specific information
wants it easy, fast, and useful

#### Other
need to update yearly
need to include electronic versions of all benefits forms

### Goals...
to create a one-stop-shop for comprehensive benefits info
to be easy to use without training or instructions
to be easy to update
to be portable so people can use it at home
to be functional, not promotional

These examples show the results of a goal-writing exercise for two different projects.

The goals of a company brochure for a diverse and possibly disinterested audience will be different from those of an employee handbook for a captive internal audience. Such differences can affect everything from how the products are delivered to the kinds of interactivity they offer.

# Which of these things is not like the others?

→ 1. A sales demo on a notebook computer in your briefcase → 2. A touchscreen kiosk about the founder of the Bank of Boise → 3. Killer Kommandos meet the Fists of Death → 4. The complete works of Shakespeare on CD-ROM

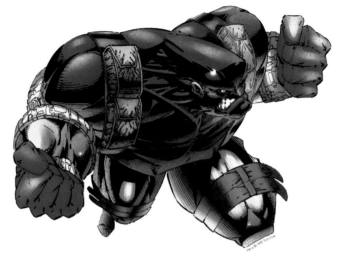

# Audience and environment

**The conditions under which an interactive product is used can influence its design as much as the content itself.**

It's fair to say that none of the products listed here have a lot in common. But before you choose Killer Kommandos as the thing that's not like the others, think about how each product is to be viewed. A kiosk, a video game, or a Shakespeare CD are likely to be used one-on-one by the viewer. A sales demo is likely to be controlled by one person (the salesperson) for another (the customer). So the sales demo calls for an entirely different class of interactivity in which the presenter controls the pace and sequence for the viewer.

Design is also influenced by the location in which a product will be used. The real world is full of distractions and noise. Or maybe the product is noisy but the user's environment is silent. Or maybe the environment is perfect but the user hasn't got a clue.

How will the answers to each of these questions affect your design? Here are a few examples:

→ A product used in someone's home can include music and narration. But a product used on a factory floor needs to rely on text, not sound.

→ A product used in schools will be run on relatively low-end computers, in contrast to a product used in business settings.

→ A product delivered over a public network can't (at today's speeds) rely on sound or video to deliver its main message, because these would take too long to download.

## → Defining conditions of use

| | | |
|---|---|---|
| **Audience** | What is the target user's ... | Age? Gender? Education? Experience with computers? |
| **Usage** | Will the product be... | Used at home? Used at work?<br>Viewed and controlled by a single person?<br>Projected in front of a group?<br>Demonstrated close-up by one person to one or more others?<br>Used just once, occasionally, or frequently? |
| **Environment** | Will the environment be... | Noisy enough to interfere with program sound?<br>Quiet, like a library or classroom?<br>Particularly bright (outdoors) or dark?<br>Unpredictable (if the display computer is portable)? |
| **Equipment** | What can you assume about... | The kind(s) of computer equipment users have?<br>The performance users' computers can deliver? |

The audience and viewing environment for your product are full of variables. You cannot always predict these and you certainly cannot control them. But you can design the product to work well under a range of probable conditions.

The next thing to do is list what you know about the audience, their equipment, and their surroundings.

# Talk to your audience.

**Audience research can be a room full of consumers answering questions from a professional moderator, and cost about $5,000 a session. Or audience research can be an evening on the phone with a few friends.**

# What do users want?

**Not everyone can afford formal user research. But no one can afford to do without any research.**

Does the idea of adding audience research to your work load seem ridiculous, or at least excessive? Do you think research is only for big companies with lots of staff and big budgets? Think again.

Whatever the size of your project and budget, it's a near certainty that you can avoid costly mistakes, and assure a better reception from your audience, if you take the time to find out what they need before you begin.

Still think you don't need research? Do you really know whether your users will want an interactive index? Searchable text? Direct access to every topic? Controls to let them print or save parts of the content?

No matter how well you know your subject and your audience, the things people tell you about their expectations and their priorities will make your product better.

# Audience research made painless

**❶** Make a list of questions to find out what users want in a product like yours:

→ What topics they look for

→ What's most and least important

→ How they would use the product

→ What similar products they liked or disliked, and why

Make sure your questions are impartial. Don't "lead" by suggesting an answer in the wording of your questions.

**❷** Choose a few people (5–10) who represent your target audience. If you don't know anyone who's an exact match for the audience, choose friends or co-workers who come close in age, interests, and so on.

**❸** Begin each interview by clearly describing the project's goals, to make sure you get responses that apply to your product.

**❹** Read your questions and write down each answer. Ask follow-up questions as necessary to get useful data. This is an informal survey, so don't worry about straying off course if your friends want to offer additional advice.

**❺** When you've made all your calls, compile the answers into a list of issues. Then analyze the implications of these issues for your project goals. You'll get remarkable insights from this exercise.

**❻** Don't be afraid to ignore parts of the advice you received if they go against your goals. The value of audience research is to validate your plans and make changes where you're off-target—not to let others do the design for you.

A note of caution about doing your own research: the best argument for hiring professional researchers, apart from their expertise, is their impartiality. Even with the best of intentions, you will naturally interpret responses according to your own biases.

So if you can't afford a pro, try to get an impartial colleague to help you analyze the advice you receive.

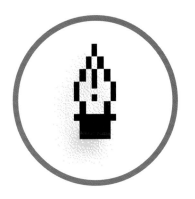  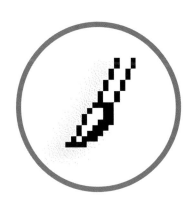 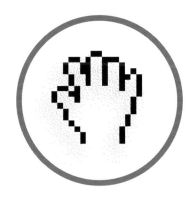

# Development choices

**What you can design depends on the medium and tool you choose. If you start with a canvas and paintbrush, you'll create something different than you would with a block of marble and a chisel. In an interactive project, these basic choices are the *medium of delivery* and the *authoring tool*.**

The medium of delivery is the technology used to get the product to its audience. The factor that most affects design is the choice between a public medium, such as the Internet, or a private medium, such as a CD-ROM or a corporation's private network.

A public network contains interactive documents published by thousands of different organizations. The reason users can seamlessly navigate among these documents is that all are authored to be compatible with standardized display software on users' computers— "browsers" such as Netscape Navigator, Mosaic, and others. This need for universal compatibility puts some restrictions on design and functionality.

In contrast, a product distributed to users on a private medium, with its own playback software, can be as unique in every way as the designer wants it to be.

# How the medium of delivery shapes design:

→ **Designing the user's experience**

**Public medium**

Products delivered via public networks consist primarily of text and images. Sound and video elements may be included in the product, but mainly as optional elements to be played only if and when the user chooses.

**Private medium**

A product on a CD-ROM or hard disk can be designed to produce a tightly integrated experience in which words, pictures, sounds, and video are combined in a particular arrangement and sequence.

→ **Designing the style and extent of interactivity**

**Public medium**

Browsers display the on-line content inside a standard document window. Both text and images can be used for navigation, but all other interaction controls are defined by the browser's menus, scroll bars, and icons.

**Private medium**

Interactive controls on the screen can be designed to have whatever look and perform whatever function the designer specifies, within the capabilities of the authoring tool.

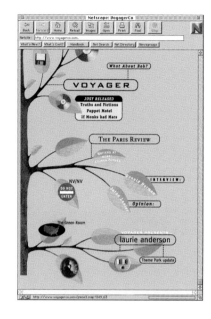

On-line delivery restricts your control over certain interface elements, but it's still possible to design an elegant interface. This on-line product catalog from Voyager contains a series of highly original and visually playful screens. There are sound and video clips, but you don't need to download these to get the message.

# The right tool for the job

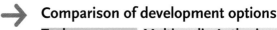

**Comparison of development options**

| Tools | Multimedia Authoring Tools |
|---|---|
| Examples | Apple Media Tool<br><br>Macromedia Director<br><br>Oracle Media Objects |
| Description | Tools for integrating text, images, sounds, and video, and sequencing these into an interactive presentation or program.<br><br>Intended for creating feature-rich and media-rich interactive products. |
| Typical Features | Usually include a high-level scripting language used to produce custom interactivity features, and to control images, sounds, video, animation, and synchronization.<br><br>Most tools include a wide variety of canned visual effects and transitions. |
| Typical Drawbacks | Steep learning curve, especially if custom scripting is needed.<br><br>Large sizes of media-rich files limit the medium of delivery to high-capacity options such as CD-ROM. |

This table illustrates the scope of influence that the authoring tool will have over design decisions. It is not an exhaustive comparison of authoring tools or their features and limitations. The examples mentioned are just a few of the many tools available.

| On-line Publishing Tools | Electronic Document Software | Presentation Software |
| --- | --- | --- |
| Hypertext Markup Language (HTML)<br><br>Tools that generate HTML documents, such as Adobe Pagemaker, Microsoft Word. | Adobe Acrobat | Adobe Persuasion<br><br>Macromedia Action<br><br>Microsoft PowerPoint |
| Provide a standardized format so documents published on-line can be compatible with browser applications used for playback.<br><br>HTML is a set of codes used to format documents for on-line publishing. A variety of editing tools are available to help in formatting HTML documents. | A document-centered approach to interactivity, based on a standard display technology to support playback on all types of computers.<br><br>Works in tandem with Internet browsers for on-line delivery of complex documents — not limited to traditional on-line design formats. | Tools for creating slide-show-style products, portable or kiosk-based demos, and projected presentations. |
| Documents can include text, images, and pointers to other files, including download-able video and sound files.<br><br>A document can be part of an infinite set of interlinked documents in any location.<br><br>Low technical skills needed for authoring (but expertise is needed to put documents on-line). | Translates documents created with any desktop publishing tool into a standard format, integrating text, graphics, and video.<br><br>Provides standardized display controls such as zooming, scrolling, and searchable text. | Most presentation tools can integrate sound and video, and provide a wide range of canned backgrounds, clip art, and special effects.<br><br>Most have extensive features for producing custom text and basic graphics such as backgrounds and borders. |
| Interactivity limited to navigation.<br><br>No control of timing, synchronization of media elements, or sequence of display.<br><br>No visual effects such as transitions. | Limited capability to customize interaction, and control sound, video, and timing. | Limited control of timing and synchronization.<br><br>Interactivity limited to navigation.<br><br>Effects and controls may not be customizable. |

# "Let's do an interactive project!"

# Raw materials

Fantasy and reality don't usually meet until the project's resources, budget, and schedule are scrutinized in the cold light of day. Creating a content inventory list is often the first reality checkpoint. The earlier you do it, the better you'll be able to predict the consequences of your design decisions. For example:

**First meeting**

→ Our customers love our products, but they think our image is…well, stodgy.

→ I know!—Let's do an interactive company brochure!

→ Yeah! We'll do a tour of the company, a video interview with the CEO—

→ And how about profiles of star employees?

→ Sure, and an overview of each division.

→ Let's get started!

**Second meeting**

→ We'd better make an inventory list of all the content we're going to need.

→ We probably have some of it already, in the annual report and data sheets and things like that.

→ Let's list all the photos, music, everything.

The "Have" vs. "Need" columns look daunting enough. But as this list shows, even the "Have" items will need work if they are not already in digital form. Art and photos have to be scanned and adjusted for digital use; text and data from different sources have to be imported and probably edited for consistency.

When you look at some of the items on your list you may decide not to include them. Just because you have video footage of something relevant, for example, doesn't mean you have to use it. Video may add nothing but expense to your project.

What you choose to put on this list—or delete from it—will depend greatly on how you're planning to deliver the product to its audience. The list in this example would be fine for an interactive brochure delivered on CD-ROM, but far too dependent on video, music, and narration if the team were directed to forget the CD and create a World Wide Web site instead.

## Third meeting

→ Know what? This is going to take a year and cost more than a corporate jet.

→ Should we forget the whole thing?

→ No! Let's just figure out what we really *need* to include.

→ **Content Inventory List for Interactive Company Brochure**

| Section | Content Item | Task | Have | Need |
|---|---|---|---|---|
| **Introduction** | Logo art | Digitize | × | |
| | Background image | Obtain and scan | | × |
| | Narration | Script, record, digitize | | × |
| | Music | Obtain and digitize | | × |
| **Company Tour** | Video | Record and digitize | | × |
| | Narration | Script, record, digitize | | × |
| | Music | Obtain and digitize | | × |
| **CEO Interview** | Video Q&A | Script, record, digitize | | × |
| **Employee Profiles** | Video of each | Record and digitize | | × |
| | Bios & info on each | Research and write | | × |
| **Division Overviews** | | | | |
| **Computers** | Staff photo | Scan annual report | × | |
| | Product photos | Scan data sheets | × | |
| | Narration | Script, record, digitize | | × |
| | Music | Obtain and digitize | | × |
| | Success stories | Research and write | | × |
| **Cameras** | Staff photo | Scan annual report | × | |
| | Product photos | Scan data sheets | × | |
| | Narration | Script, record, digitize | | × |
| | Music | Obtain and digitize | | × |
| | Success stories | Research and write | | × |
| **Copiers** | Staff photo | Obtain and scan | | × |
| | Product photos | Scan data sheets | × | |
| | Narration | Script, record, digitize | | × |
| | Music | Obtain and digitize | | × |
| | Success stories | Research and write | | × |

> "When we started this training CD one year ago, we actually had eight weeks scheduled for it—that's how little we knew." —Training manager, Major corporation

## Cause and effect

**This decision:**
We need original theme music for the interactive company brochure

**Has these project plan implications:**
Hire a composer
Hire musicians
Rent a recording studio
Hire an audio engineer
Record the original music
Mix and edit the audio tracks
Obtain audio digitizing hardware
Obtain audio editing software
Convert the music to digital format
Edit sound for levels, timing, fades, etc.
Integrate music into presentation
Synchronize music with visuals

# Planning

**When you venture into new territory, it's impossible to set out fully prepared. But if you haven't figured out how much time and money it will take to get where you want to go, you may run out of both before you get there.**

By now you've made some key decisions about the project's goals, audience, delivery medium, authoring tool, and content. How do all these pieces fit together? How can you make sure that what you're setting out to do is practical, or even possible? Your next job is to create a project plan—to be accountant and project manager as well as designer.

Depending on the kind of project you're doing, a project plan can take many forms.

The most important aspect of planning is thinking through all the implications of what you're setting out to do. What are all the tasks ahead? How long will they take? How much will they cost? Do you have the right equipment? Do you have people with the right skills?

It's tempting at every point along the way to jump in and start designing screens. But the project will go more smoothly if the plan drives the design, not the other way around.

## Trouble?

Some aspects of any plan are so likely to cause problems that it's a good idea to avoid them if possible—or, if they can't be avoided, to adjust the schedule and budget accordingly.
The "red flag" list:

→ Collaborating with co-workers in distant locations (unless you all do this daily).

→ Relying on hardware or software you've never used before.

→ Signing up for tasks you've never done before.

→ Using a significant amount of content for which permissions are needed.

→ Producing original audio, video, or animation (unless you already know how).

→ Needing buy-in or reviews from a large group of people, or from busy top-level executives.

→ Accepting significant hardware or media constraints (for example, the product must fit on a floppy disk).

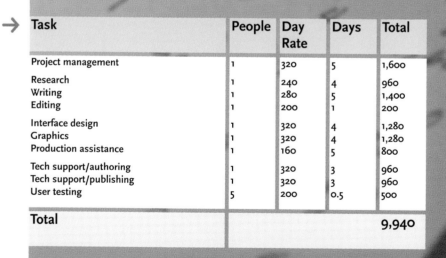

## Task and budget projection for a simple interactive document

This projection of tasks and costs is just one example of many possible planning tools. Your objective in making this kind of projection is to understand the big picture, not to account for every detail.

A simple project like the one in this example might be done by half a dozen people working on nothing else for two weeks. Or it might be done by one or two people diverting time from other jobs over the course of one or two months. The tasks represent work categories, and not necessarily work sequence. Many tasks are done simultaneously on a real project.

Even if you aren't paying the team members directly, estimating their day rates (based on either their hourly salaries or the going rates for contract work in your area) can help you demonstrate what the project really "costs" to create.

| Task | People | Day Rate | Days | Total |
|---|---|---|---|---|
| Project management | 1 | 320 | 5 | 1,600 |
| Research | 1 | 240 | 4 | 960 |
| Writing | 1 | 280 | 5 | 1,400 |
| Editing | 1 | 200 | 1 | 200 |
| Interface design | 1 | 320 | 4 | 1,280 |
| Graphics | 1 | 320 | 4 | 1,280 |
| Production assistance | 1 | 160 | 5 | 800 |
| Tech support/authoring | 1 | 320 | 3 | 960 |
| Tech support/publishing | 1 | 320 | 3 | 960 |
| User testing | 5 | 200 | 0.5 | 500 |
| **Total** | | | | **9,940** |

goals
audience needs
environment

content
lists
categories

structure
access
flowchart

# Organization

**Organizing information means more than just sorting it into categories. At the heart of every design project are value-laden questions such as "How should this material be prioritized?" "What does the audience need to know about this subject?" and "What do they want to do with the information?"**

The project definition tasks leading to this point have helped to identify the content you'll be working with, but how does this content become an interface? How do the things you've learned about the audience translate into facts about how they'll use the product? What will be their highest-priority topics? What types of access and links between topics will they need?

The answers to these questions take shape as the content is arranged into topics and groups. As you begin to visualize the information being used in various ways, put yourself in the role of the user and see how the possible content structures might work. It will become apparent where a link might be needed, or that two groups should be combined, or that access to a topic makes more sense from one group than another.

# Simplicity

William of Ockham, a medieval philosopher known for many contributions to modern thought, is often cited for his Principle of Parsimony, stating that economy or simplicity is the essence of a good explanation. This principle is known today as Ockham's Razor, and it applies as well to 20th-century information design as it did to 14th-century science.

Most collections of information tend to have natural internal structures of their own. As you begin to work with your own material, you may see categories emerge on the basis of

→ theme or topic

→ size or scale

→ geographic location

→ historical sequence

→ narrative sequence

If you're converting an existing product such as an employee handbook or a company annual report, you may already have a basic structure for the content. That structure may work fine when the product is converted to digital form, and if it does, there's no reason to change it. But don't reproduce the structure of an existing product without asking whether interactivity provides ways to improve on it.

For example, there may be opportunities to add value by improving information access and usability:

→ providing direct links between related topics

→ providing easy and flexible ways to search the content

→ reorganizing content to support how it will be accessed and used

# Equipment you'll need:

a pen

paper

tacks

a wall

# The organization exercise

### Step 1: List all possible content categories.

These categories will come from several sources: the existing product or materials you have to work with, your audience research, your content inventory, and your imagination.

The goal is to generate a comprehensive list of content categories for the project. Don't worry about redundancy or the fact that big and small categories are all mixed up together. You'll organize and prune in the coming steps.

### Step 2: Start to group things by topic.

Begin by identifying the obvious meta-categories, which will become the top-level subjects that users see first.

Then start to move topics from the master list to sublists. Create only one level of sublists at this point (no sub-sublists), or you'll risk getting bogged down in small details at the expense of the larger picture.

### Step 3: Refine the topic groups.

Move topics around on the sublists until they work. This is an iterative, trial-and-error process. You'll probably discover that some items don't seem to fit in any category, while others fit in more than one (see example at right).

Not all lists yield natural categories. Part of your job as designer may be to fabricate categories (such as, "who's who" or "commonly asked questions").

Master content list for an interactive employee benefits guide. The master list is a holding tank for all content categories, which will be refined and moved onto sublists that represent the project's main topics.

## Master List

| | | |
|---|---|---|
| salary | bonuses | termination |
| 401K | workplace policies | health |
| stock options | ethics | workplace injuries |
| vacation | medical benefits | disability insurance |
| sabbatical | maternity | disability policy |
| fitness center | leaves of absence | |
| retirement plan | reviews | |

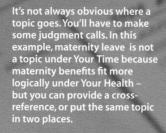

It's not always obvious where a topic goes. You'll have to make some judgment calls. In this example, maternity leave is not a topic under Your Time because maternity benefits fit more logically under Your Health – but you can provide a cross-reference, or put the same topic in two places.

| Your Time | Your Money | Your Health | Your Work |
|---|---|---|---|
| work hours | salary | medical benefits | workplace policies |
| vacation | bonuses | maternity | ethics |
| sabbatical | stock options | fitness center | harrassment |
| leaves of absence | 401K | workplace injuries | reviews |
| | retirement plan | disability insurance | termination |
| | loans | disability policy | |

**Top-down hierarchy**

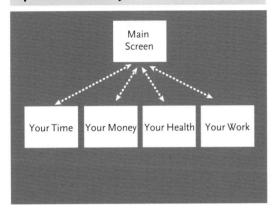

**Hierarchical web**

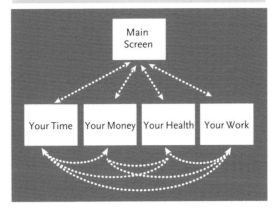

This is the most common and simplest structure. Access is provided from a central entry point—a "main menu"—down to each principal topic area. Moving from one topic area to another requires a step back to the main menu. In a product where users stay within a single topic for an extended time, this step back can serve as a useful "top view" of the topics.

Since this employee benefits example would be used for reference, users may frequently skip around within topics and find the extra step of returning to the main menu cumbersome.

The web structure provides the same access as the top-down hierarchy at left, with the added option of direct access to any major topic from any other topic.

**Step 4:  Arrange the groups into a structure.**
The arrangement of the groups represents not just organization, but access. So while this step is similar in many ways to the outlining you've done for paper documents, there's one notable difference: the arrangement is not sequential. You need to design one or more specific paths leading to every item.

As you try out different arrangements, you'll see that some work better than others, as in the example above.

The most critical requirement of this process is making sure that the topic categories are well defined and clearly distinct from each other. If the topics overlap, users will be confused about where to find what they need.

Choosing a particular kind of information structure is not the goal of this exercise. What's important is to be aware, as you create groups and the relationships among them, that the structure you produce needs to be coherent and well balanced to result in a product that's easy to navigate.

The structure you design here is the beginning of the product's flowchart—the object of the information design process.

## Structure as an editorial tool

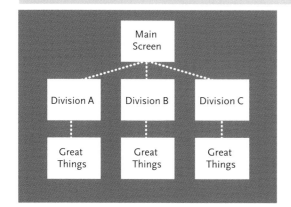

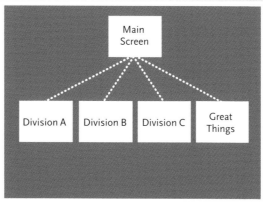

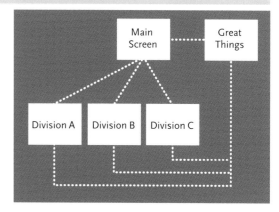

Here's part of a structure for an interactive company brochure. Among its goals are

→ to introduce each of the company's divisions

→ to highlight the major accomplishments of each division

Since one of the goals is to spotlight major accomplishments, they are moved into a section that can be accessed directly from the main screen. But this solution raises a new problem: moving the "Great Things" category up the hierarchy has eliminated the accomplishments from each division.

To solve this problem, the new section remains available at the top level, but a new link is added for access from each division.

# The invisible hand of structure

As information designer, you are a gatekeeper. Even though users make their own choices, it's up to you what choices they have—what they see first, where they can go, and what they don't see at all.

How you arrange the content determines how easy it is to get to every piece of information. And making it easier, faster, and more direct to get to one topic or another inevitably creates a point of view. There is nothing wrong with imposing a point of view—the designer's point of view is often what makes a product interesting. It only becomes a problem when the designer inadvertently creates bias by arranging topics in a way that implies priority.

Consider an on-line corporate information site with three content categories: Company History, Products, and Management. Suppose someone decided to add the latest version of the annual report, but didn't want to create a new section for it—so they put it under Company History. Such compromises make it unlikely that users will find the "misfiled" information, except by accident.

# What every flowchart needs

There are no firm rules about how a flowchart must look, as long as it works as a clear map to your information design.

The structure of this flowchart is typical. The elements shown—hierarchical levels and links—are necessary to make the flowchart easily understood by anyone who might read it.

A flowchart gives shape and structure to the content so people can get a sense of how the real product might work. It is a living document that you will return to throughout the project, as the basis for decisions about structure and navigation.

# The flowchart

**An information flowchart is simply an outline presented as a box diagram, with lines that show the access routes among its parts. The ideal flowchart is a clear, easy-to-follow specification of a project's topic categories, levels, and links.**

Designing a good flowchart requires common sense and careful attention to details. No matter how simple or straightforward your project seems, it still needs a flowchart. Diagramming the content will show you things about organization and access that you wouldn't otherwise know—and the later in the design process you discover problems with organization and access, the harder and more expensive it will be to fix them.

Three forces drive the design of a flowchart:

→ Content: The organization and structure you've mapped out for the information.

→ Usability: The topic categories and access routes the audience will expect to find.

→ Simplicity: The need to keep the design clear and focused, to control production time and costs.

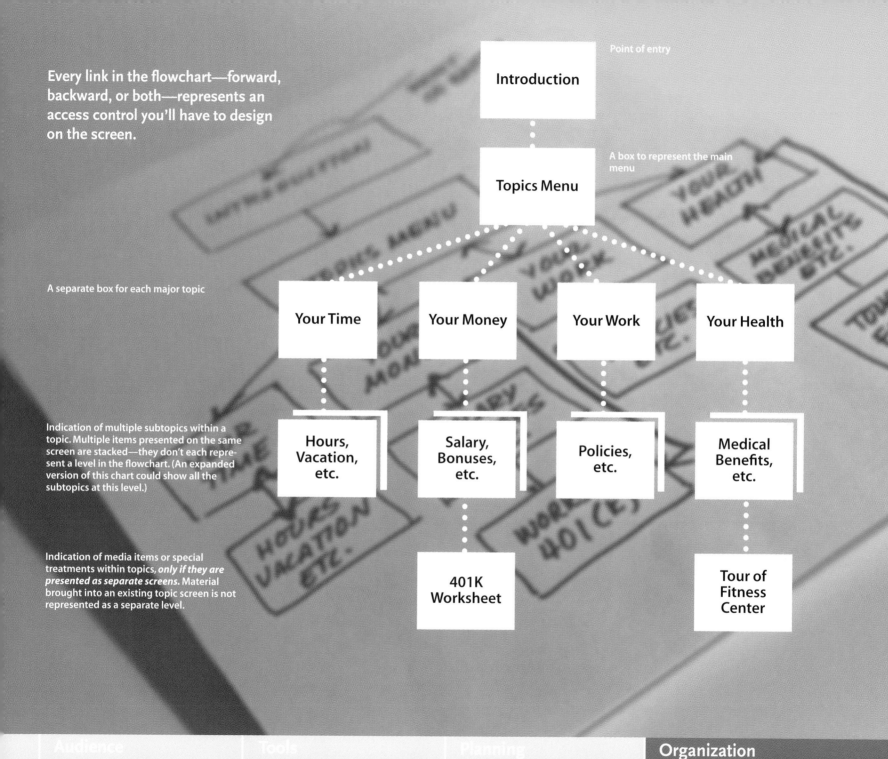

Every link in the flowchart—forward, backward, or both—represents an access control you'll have to design on the screen.

Point of entry

**Introduction**

A box to represent the main menu

**Topics Menu**

A separate box for each major topic

**Your Time**

**Your Money**

**Your Work**

**Your Health**

Indication of multiple subtopics within a topic. Multiple items presented on the same screen are stacked—they don't each represent a level in the flowchart. (An expanded version of this chart could show all the subtopics at this level.)

**Hours, Vacation, etc.**

**Salary, Bonuses, etc.**

**Policies, etc.**

**Medical Benefits, etc.**

Indication of media items or special treatments within topics, *only if they are presented as separate screens.* Material brought into an existing topic screen is not represented as a separate level.

**401K Worksheet**

**Tour of Fitness Center**

goals
content
flowchart

interaction

Part Two

navigation
access
functionality

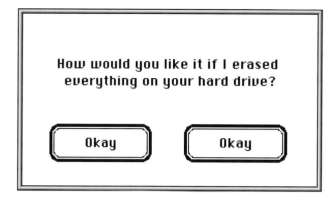

How would you like it if I erased
everything on your hard drive?

Okay     Okay

**A favorite example of the power of interactivity, from a media design studio called Mackerel. If you reach this message in their demo, you can't leave without clicking one of the two buttons. They're just kidding, of course, but it's impossible to click "Okay" without feeling a twinge of terror.**

# Interaction Design

**This is where you start building the machine. Part One focused on planning the design and answered the question, "What is this product?" Part Two focuses on the mechanics of the design and answers the question, "How should it work?"**

Interactivity in a computer product means that the user, not the designer, controls the sequence, the pace, and most importantly, what to look at and what to ignore.

But simply "putting the user in charge" opens up an infinite range of possibilities: in charge of exactly what? This is the starting point of interaction design—deciding exactly where and how to give control to users.

The prospect of designing interaction is often met with apprehension about technology: people expect this process to require expertise about computers. And while it helps to know what computers can do, most of what you're designing is human, not technical—successful interaction means a person telling a computer what to do, and not the other way around. Figuring out what the user wants to do at any given time is the basis of all interaction design.

# Critical tasks of interaction design

→ Create a guidance system to orient users
→ Design the navigation and access routes
→ Define what happens in every screen
→ Design controls for interaction
→ Create a storyboard

**How does an information design become an interaction design? The tasks listed above represent the steps in that process. Starting with the information flowchart, you create the features that allow users to travel through and manipulate the content.**

In the process of interaction design you are turning the flowchart, which shows only content and structure, into a storyboard, which shows pathways and controls as well.

In other words, moving from information design to interaction design means turning information into an experience.

At the big-picture level, this means

→ motivating users to *have* the experience, by giving them clear guidance and options

→ creating an interesting journey—or at least a clear path—through the information

→ giving users controls that allow them to go where they want and do what they want

→ making the experience as easy and intuitive as possible

## → How much interaction?

| Slide Show ← ← ← | | | | | → → → Full-immersion virtual reality | | |
|---|---|---|---|---|---|---|
| **Control Pace** | **Control Sequence** | **Control Media** | **Control Variables** | **Control Transaction** | **Control Objects** | **Control Simulation** |
| Click when you're ready to advance to the next thing | Choose where you want to go at any time | Start/stop video; search text; scroll/ zoom the view | Change the outcome of a chart; customize a database search | Enter a password; pay a bill; send a message | Move things around screen; shoot ducks; behead opponents | Change the perspective of view, or the course of events/action |

This continuum represents the range of possible user interaction and specifies the kinds of things that users can control. It's a vocabulary of interaction that can help you express your goals in basic terms.

In any project, the interaction design is partly a function of development time, money, and technical resources. The more interactive control you give to users, the more complex the product will be to develop.

But how much and what type of interaction is needed really depends on the content itself: what sort of interactive experience are you setting out to deliver?

→ A simple interactive document may need only basic navigation and media controls.

→ An electronic catalog may need database search and transaction capabilities.

→ A medical training course might need not only navigation and media controls, but also control over instrument "objects" and realistic 3-D surgical simulations.

The methods used to create each product would be quite different. But whatever the level of interaction, the basic goals of interaction design remain the same: clarity, simplicity, and ease of use.

A book has a table of contents, chapters, and page numbers. You can pick it up and quickly get a sense of its length, contents, and style.

Newspapers and magazines are filled with headlines, photos, and captions for instant scanning. You can easily grasp their contents and read only the parts that look interesting.

Movies use quick cuts, fades, dissolves, and countless other devices to signal changes in time, location, and even mood.

# Orientation

**The immediate frustration with an interactive product is that you cannot pick it up, thumb through it, and determine its usefulness. Whether users can get what they need (and often whether they invest the time to find out) depends on getting them oriented right from the start.**

People expect the friendly, familiar paradigms of media to guide them through uncharted territories of information. As children they learn to open books and turn their pages, and later to pause at each blackout of their favorite TV show for the inevitable "word from our sponsor." Each medium brings with it a unique language of orientation.

These guidance systems have become widely standardized and understood—until now. Interactive products present such a Babel of orientation and navigation models that standards may take many years to evolve. The challenge is to produce designs that are intuitive and easy to use, even in the absence of well-known paradigms.

# Give users the lay of the land.

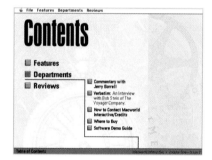

To give people their bearings in an information product, the first screens need to tell them what they're going to do, see, or experience. What's needed is a balance of images and words that provide enough guidance to be useful, without an overwhelming amount of detail.

Unlike movie audiences or users of computer games, users of information products want to know exactly what's in the product and where to find it.

Many approaches to orientation are possible. A company information site might use simple images and captions to introduce itself, suggesting that a casual and entertaining browse lies ahead. A more complex or extensive product might need a more versatile orientation scheme, providing multiple levels of information about the content so that users can see as much or as little detail as they want.

### Image map

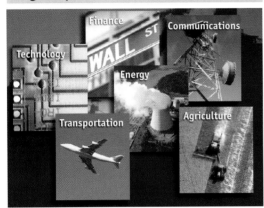

An image map uses images to represent content literally. The user just selects a topic to find out more about it.

### Metaphor

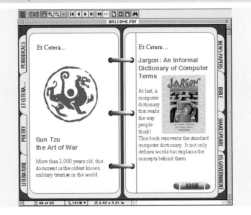

The familiar looseleaf notebook gives users an intuitive method of getting around—by clicking section tabs—as well as an immediate overview of the content by showing all the categories at once.

# Image maps and metaphors

**A natural place to get users oriented is the main navigation screen. Whether it's called a main menu, a home page, or something else, it has the same purpose: to set up the conceptual space in which users will navigate. When that space is made up of images that lead to parts of the content, it's called an image map.**

An image map has two purposes: the images both represent and lead to the content. Any collection of images can be an image map—separate items or one integrated picture; images with or without words. The concern at this point in the design process isn't creating the images, but defining the concepts that will introduce users to the content.

A metaphor is a special kind of image map that places images in a meaningful context, by presenting information in terms of an object (like a book), a location (like an office building), or a device (like a VCR) that people already use outside the computer environment.

A metaphor can only work—that is, make access to a product easier—if the audience is familiar with it, and if it's a good conceptual fit for the content.

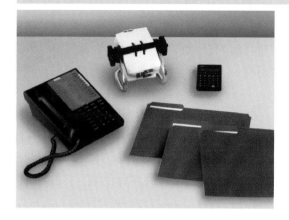

Navigational or functional metaphor? This is a functional metaphor. Each item leads to a tool: calculator, address book, and so on.

Metaphor or image map? This is an image map. Each item leads to a part of the content, but there's no overarching context for the picture.

Good or bad metaphor? The whole point of a metaphor is to create meaning. If you have to ask what the meaning is, the metaphor isn't working.

# The right metaphor:

→ Does it help viewers understand what to do?

→ Is it appropriate for the content?

→ Are there any parts of the content that clearly won't fit the metaphor?

→ Does the metaphor create audience expectations you can't meet?

Metaphors are not just for complex multimedia programs or games. For example, to get information about medical procedures, users might click instruments arranged in an on-screen doctor's office. This is a navigational metaphor: the doctor's office provides a familiar context to make the search for information less abstract.

A functional metaphor, in contrast, creates an environment in which objects perform the functions they depict. The best-known example is the familiar desktop metaphor of many computer interfaces, where folders are places to file documents, trash cans are places to throw things away, and an electronic address book holds names and addresses.

Functional metaphors represent a level of interactivity that's found more often in software applications and high-end multimedia than in simple information products. But navigational metaphors can work in almost any information product.

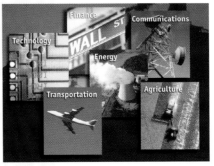

## Separating content from overhead

Since a product's main navigation screen (main menu or home page) is the gateway to the content, it's used more often than any other screen. So a problem arises if this screen is used for "housekeeping" items (things the user does once or infrequently): the screen ends up hosting many chores that have nothing to do with navigation.

Examples of housekeeping items:

→ setting preferences

→ product registration or sign-in

→ credits

The illustrations show one way to simplify the main navigation screen: separate housekeeping items from the content by putting them on a different introductory screen. Then the main navigation screen doesn't need to be cluttered with items that are rarely used.

# Navigation

**In many interactive products, the user's primary form of interaction is navigating through the content. It follows that much of interaction design is really navigation design: creating interfaces that help people understand where they are, where they can go, and how to get there.**

An information flowchart defines a product's structure, so once a flowchart exists, a lot of navigation design work has already been done. The next step is to design the access routes between topics and the controls that users interact with. As a result of this process, the flowchart will probably change—for the better.

A good navigation design will

→ Minimize travel: create the simplest and shortest path between any two points

→ Minimize depth: create a hierarchy with the fewest possible levels (extra levels mean extra travel steps)

→ Minimize redundancy: avoid creating multiple paths to the same place from the same screen (this causes confusion about which to choose)

How is an access route different from the links already shown in the flowchart? The flowchart typically shows *direct* links between adjacent levels and topics. But an access route could also be created, for example, by a Main Menu button on a screen three layers down, which would bring the user back to the Main Menu in one click. Designing navigation means specifying *all* the routes.

# Every link in your flowchart represents an access route you'll need to create

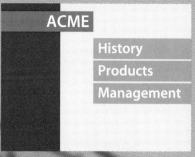

Every screen needs controls that take users forward to the places they can go, and back to the places they came from. From this main screen, users need access only downward to topics.

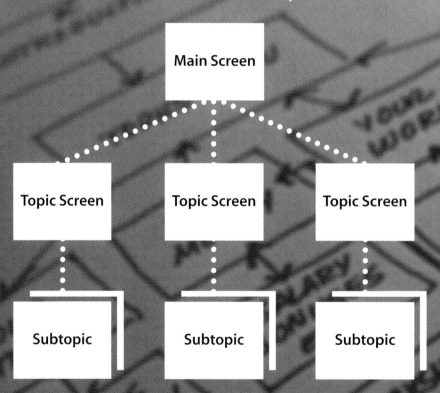

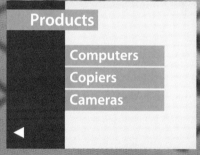

The topic screen provides access in two directions: down to individual subtopics, and back up to the main screen.

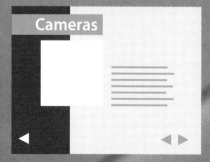

The next level of access is sideways—between items within the same subtopic. Access back to the topic screen is still available.

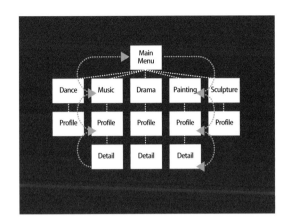

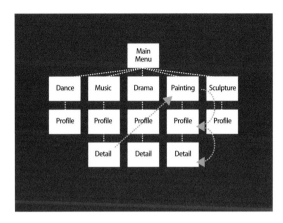

In this example, moving from one detail screen to another in a different topic takes six steps. It's possible that the flowchart has too many layers and could be condensed. But if not, a solution can be found by changing the access route rather than the structure.

One way to change the access route is to take the list of main topics with you wherever you go. Keeping these on the screen at all times can be a convenient express route.

Having the product's main topics accessible from the detail screen has cut the number of travel steps in half.

# Direct access

Your goal is to provide the simplest path between any two points in the product. This means minimizing the number of travel steps, as well as the perceived difficulty, in getting from one place to another.

# Types of access

Just as information can be organized to suggest a point of view (see page 31), access methods can also tell a story.

There are many different access solutions: menus, lists, timelines, icons, buttons, maps. Entirely different methods can be used to provide access to the same content.

In an interactive product designed to highlight major corporate accomplishments, a simple way to give users access is to organize the material into topic categories, each available by way of a button.

If the intent of the product is also to recognize outstanding achievers, major accomplishments can be featured instead through profiles of the people whose efforts were most significant.

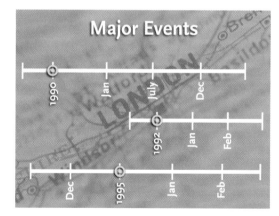

Or, if the intent is to convey a sense of history and progress, access can be provided by means of a timeline showing the major events along a spectrum of months or years.

Screens 1 and 2 are main topic screens from an educational program. While there is an obvious stylistic resemblance between them, the elements they contain are completely different, because the content they cover is different.

The two lower screens are subtopics of screens 1 and 2, respectively. Each subtopic screen retains many design elements of the corresponding topic screen, to make it clear that the user is still in the same space.

# Levels of access

There are two levels of access:

→ Access to a new topic: Going to a new topic can be a major leap and a complete change of scene.

→ Access within a topic: Bringing up new material within the same topic should be as subtle as possible, to keep the user anchored and in control.

**1**

**2**

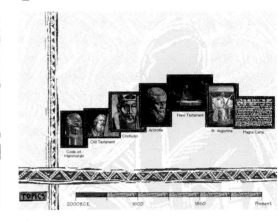

Few things cause as much traveler's anxiety as products that jump from screen to screen to screen, leaving the user wondering, "Where am I?" or "How am I ever going to get back?"

There's a simple solution that helps keep users oriented and also reduces the number of screens you'll need to design: bring new material to the current screen, rather than sending users to a new screen.

Here's an example: Because documents on public networks use a system of links that typically lead to new pages, users can easily become disoriented while traveling within a document. But if the new pages retain visual anchors such as headlines, backgrounds, and other key graphics, users perceive that new material has been brought to the current location, not that they have traveled to a new location.

# The price of a link

It's often considered desirable to provide a rich system of cross-links among topics. But each link carries a design price tag:

→ If the link sends the user to a new location, access controls need to be created so the user can return without getting lost.

→ If the link brings material from another topic to the current screen, the content may need to be redesigned to work in the new location.

For example:

→ If a user clicked on a link in Screen A, bringing to this screen some content that had originally been designed for Screen B, the new content could fit in without problems.

→ If the link in Screen A referred to content found on Screen C, this content could not be brought to Screen A without significant redesign. The user would have to be sent to Screen C, then brought back.

**HISTORY**

A

**EXPLORERS**

B

Revolution

C

# Random access: less is more

**Random access and links between topics are two of the defining features of interactive products. But complete freedom of access with unlimited links can create confusion for users and design problems for you.**

Net surfing, or browsing among the millions of documents published on-line, is by definition the act of following links. It's easy to get lost or to forget where in the chain of links an item of interest was located, but the overall experience is consistent with browsing: people don't expect an integrated look and feel or a sense of continuity among all those documents.

But having unlimited access and diversity *among* documents doesn't relieve the designer of having to maintain continuity and a sense of direction *within* a document.

Whether a product is distributed on-line, on CD-ROM, or by any other medium, the goal of designing access routes and links is to make navigation as simple and direct as possible.

The sphere of the self's power is simply the sphere of what happens well. It is the entire unoffending and obedient part of the world. —Santayana

**A few examples that violate key principles of usability:**

→ Conflicting controls for similar operations

→ Cryptic messages

→ "Creative" redefinition of standard interface elements, such as menus that pop out of buttons

→ Excessive and redundant media controls

# Usability

**Designing usability is not a step in the interface design process—it's not something you do once and never think about again. It is an ongoing part of the design process.**

An interface is intuitive only if it behaves the way people expect it to, and it can do that only if the designer was capable of anticipating what assumptions people would make about the product's behavior.

Interactive products that are considered intuitive and easy to use have had a lot of design effort invested in anticipating, understanding, and managing users' expectations.

Luckily for you, users will bring many helpful expectations with them to the product. They will expect a mouse click to take them somewhere or show them something; they will expect icons they've seen elsewhere to do what they've done elsewhere. This doesn't mean that all interaction must be familiar. New kinds of interaction may be better, as long as they make sense to users.

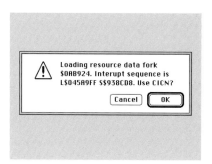

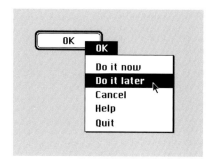

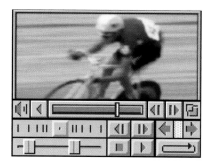

Beyond relying on common sense to judge a product's ease of use, there are specific steps you can take to anticipate and avoid usability problems. These steps don't make up a formal process, but rather a set of guidelines with which to approach every design decision and review. The next few pages describe these usability guidelines.

**Some basic things to keep in mind**
Users of your product are trying to do, find, or learn something. Your job is to make their job as easy as possible, and get out of their way.

If you strip out every interaction feature that's not critical and aim for complete simplicity, the number of people who thank you will far outnumber those who say they would have liked more features.

→ Don't add to their burden by making them "learn" to use your product.

→ Don't make them do things the product could do for itself (starting video, playing sounds) unless they need to control these.

→ Don't waste their time with elaborate features or multiple ways of doing things.

## Remove obstacles

In this picture, the labels are an unnecessary and artificial layer between the viewer and the content. There's no reason to use menus or lists when the topics are clearly represented on the screen. Just let the user click the object of interest.

## Minimize effort

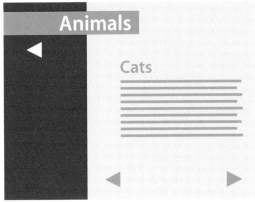

People need to cover a lot of screen territory to navigate through this product. Navigation is easier when related buttons are grouped together.

## Give feedback

The buttons at the top of this screen are used to move between the topics in the program. But although one of the buttons represents the current topic, it doesn't look any different from the others. Dimming this button, as shown below, would make it clear that the other three topics can still be selected.

## Remove obstacles

A good interactive product doesn't get in the user's way. It doesn't use elaborate guidance schemes and symbols, and it doesn't try to explain itself or to direct the user's activities, unless the user wants it to.

One way to remove obstacles is to let people interact with the content as directly as possible. Let them click the things they want to find out about, and give them simple express routes to the information they're looking for.

## Minimize effort

Users shouldn't get the feeling that simply moving around the screen is work. You can minimize their effort by keeping related controls close together, and by putting frequently used buttons in places that are easy to reach in relation to other items on the screen. For example, in a reference product where someone might often be paging forward and backward, the Next and Previous buttons shouldn't be on opposite sides of the screen.

## Give feedback

Most people assume that when a computer seems to be doing nothing, it is, in fact, doing nothing. If a product doesn't respond in some way to a user's action, the user will think the action hasn't registered. Feedback should be both appropriate and immediate—for example, responding to mouse clicks with a "mouse click" (or other) sound, and highlighting items that have been selected.

### Be explicit

Which devices are active? Tape, stapler, calculator ... ? The only way to tell is to click them all.

### Be flexible

Introductions and demonstrations are often necessary—once. There should always be a way to skip or interrupt them.

### Be forgiving

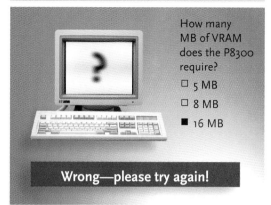

At this point a user might simply quit or walk away. Even in instructional settings, where the user may have no choice but to work through the entire program, it's more helpful to add hints or a way to view the part of the program where the answer can be found.

## Be explicit

Make it obvious what is clickable on the screen and what is not. Objects that look like buttons should act like buttons. If images have hot areas, make sure they are distinct from the rest of the image.

Certain tools for viewing interactive products, such as on-line document browsers, provide options to automatically indicate clickable text and images, and to highlight these when they are selected.

## Be flexible

Users will expect the product to let them take shortcuts, so they can skip things they've seen before and go directly to wherever they think the action is. They will also expect to leave things that don't interest them—instantly. Make all media (sound, movies, animation) interruptible. Make it easy to quit at any time, from anywhere, by using the computer's standard keyboard shortcuts for quitting.

## Be forgiving

Users will expect the product to let them do whatever they want, with no restrictions or penalties. They will make mistakes, change their minds, and generally expect the product to compensate. Don't create conditions where users have to "do the right thing" before they can move on—for example, by not letting them leave a screen until they choose a correct response, or by making them type a word correctly to search for a topic.

# Functionality

Like usability, functionality isn't tied to just one step in the design process. It's been part of the picture since the earliest stages of product definition. But it comes into focus now because the storyboard—the big milestone of interaction design—will require you to nail down every functionality decision.

Designing functionality means specifying in detail what has been vague up to this point. It's a reality check that forces you to reexamine earlier assumptions about the content and what can be done with it, and to change the design until problems are solved.

Designing functionality also means watching the trees and the forest at the same time.

It's the process of looking at both the closeup view of individual controls that users interact with, and the big picture of how all the controls in the product work together.

Finally, designing functionality means asking a lot of questions and testing different answers until you find the ones that work best in the storyboard.

# Designing functionality:
# A macro view

These are the big-picture issues of function-ality. Each represents design decisions that are part of defining how the product will work. Each has to be considered at the level of individual screens, as well as at the level of the whole product.

### Defining interaction controls

Designing controls for interaction means defining not only *what* happens on each individual screen, but *how*: how users get there, how they leave, and all the actions they can take in between. While the specific controls for interaction are dictated by the immediate goals of each screen, the product's overall functionality should be developed as a system of well integrated parts.

### Solving organizational problems

Solving organizational problems means addressing the many inconsistencies inherent in the content: even with your best efforts, no body of information can be perfectly organized or uniformly distributed. Every collection of data has a few items that are too long or too short, or that need special treatment, a different access route, and so on.

### Ensuring consistency

Consistency in all the ways a product behaves makes the experience of using it more intuitive, and allows users to learn the fewest possible new behaviors. For example, if one part of a product offers the option to hear on-screen text read by a narrator, users will expect to find the same option when they move to a new topic.

### Managing dependencies

In any product, there are dependencies created by relationships among different screens. An example is the dependency created by the sequence in which screens are viewed. If a product's main menu were to display a checkmark to indicate each section the user had completed, this feature would affect decisions about creating direct links between sections and bypassing that main menu.

### Controlling media and custom features

The controls users interact with represent only part of a product's functionality. The rest is the product's own behavior at any time: how it controls text, images, and sounds; and how it performs any custom functions that may be part of the design. Every individual decision that goes into defining these controls is part of designing functionality.

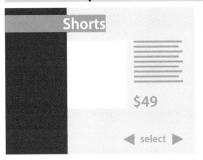

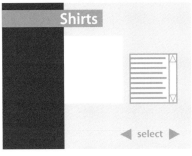

The real danger in designing controls late in the game, or one screen at a time, is that content exceptions can make hash of an otherwise simple and sensible design. The way to solve the problems here is to back off from designing individual screens and controls, and to "worst-case" the content before going any further. This means identifying the content items that differ from the others in any significant ways, and coming up with functionality solutions that will work for them, as well as for the more typical items.

This clothing catalog is a straightforward database of items with a picture, description, and price for each one. This screen example shows the basic elements for a typical item.

The second item has too much text to fit on one screen, so a scroll bar has been added. Does this solve the problem? Now users can't see the price of the item without scrolling to the end of the text. And what about shorter items? Should the scroll bar stay there for consistency, or go away when it isn't needed?

The next item is a monogrammed shirt. The user needs a way to type her initials. There's no room for that, so a second page is added. How does she get to the second page? Those arrows are there to move between items. Should there really be a special case just for this item? And how does the user get back to the first page?

# Solving functionality problems: A micro view

Here are a few examples of common interaction design problems and their solutions. While the solutions may look simple, these types of problems often affect screens throughout a product.

## Status Confusion—"What mode am I in?"

| Specs | **Features** |
|-------|-------|

→ **Blazing performance**
→ **Chrome alloy wheels**
→ **Ten-speed CD-ROM drive**
→ **30-day battery**
→ **Weighs less than six ounces!**

### Features

→ **Blazing performance**
→ **Chrome alloy wheels**
→ **Ten-speed CD-ROM drive**
→ **30-day battery**
→ **Weighs less than six ounces!**

Specs

### Specs

→ **1000 MHz 88880 CPR**
→ **128 GB HD**
→ **256 MB REM**
→ **512 SX3 GaO2 nano**
→ **Waterproof to 500 meters**

Features

Is the screen above showing Specs, or Features? Users might guess that the brighter button indicates the current state, but in this case it shows the alternate state they can select. The opposite state is just as likely to be misunderstood. The only sure solution to this common problem is to avoid showing both buttons at once. The two-screen version of the information, at right, prevents this confusion.

## Function Confusion—"What does this button do?"

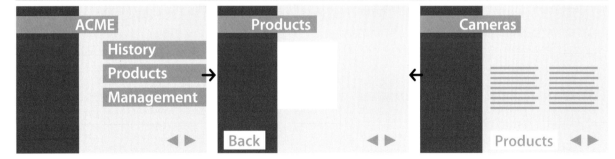

If users generally travel to the Products screen from the menu above, they will expect the "Back" button to bring them back to that menu. But if a link gives access to the Products screen from somewhere else, what should the "Back" button do? Ideally, a button's function should never change, but if that rule is enforced here, the button will need to be renamed "Menu."

# Built-in or custom controls?

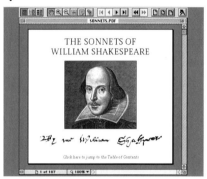

Acrobat Reader, the free browser used to display Adobe Acrobat digital documents, provides interaction controls for scrolling, paging, zooming, and other features. Acrobat Exchange, the retail browser, adds full-text search, video and sound, hypertext link creation, and a plug-in architecture. These capabilities are built in so designers can create functionality without scripting or programming.

Designing customized interaction controls can mean programming. But not all products need custom controls. An increasing number of authoring and viewing tools provide built-in interaction controls that can be added by people without engineering skills.

# Controlling video, sound, and text: A micro view

→ **Video control decisions**

| How does it start? | How does it end? | How much control? | What control device? |
|---|---|---|---|
| Is the video window always on the screen, or does it appear only when needed? The answer depends on how video is used in different sections of your product. If it's an integral part of the presentation, video should appear and begin automatically at the appropriate moment. If it's there for enhancement or diversion, let the user click the movie window or a control to start it. | When the movie ends, you can leave up the last frame, replace it with a poster frame, or remove the video window altogether. Don't leave an empty window on the screen—it's ugly, and takes up space you could use for something else. | Given the product and its content, how much user control is appropriate? Users should always be able to interrupt. But will they want to restart? And if so, should they restart where they left off, or back at the beginning? Will they want to replay the movie one or more times? Will they want to move between single frames? | The appropriate control device depends on the level of user control. It can be as simple as clicking the movie to start or stop. If more explicit control is needed and your resources and authoring tool permit, custom-designed controls are generally easier to integrate visually than the built-in controller bars of digital video software. |

→ **Sound control decisions**

| How does it start? | How does it end? | Continuity? | How much control? |
|---|---|---|---|
| Background music, sound effects, and introductory narrations are typically initiated by the program. Users may need to start sound or narration that is informational or instructional. | If the user chooses another topic or moves to another screen before the sound ends, should the sound stop, or fade out? Fading is usually more graceful, but you may need to experiment, especially with juxtaposed sounds that may be jarring. | If there are multiple screens in the section, does sound continue as the user moves between them? This would be fine for music, but narrations may need to be keyed to each segment. | How much control do users need? Users should always be able to turn the volume down or off. In addition, depending on the content, they may need to stop and restart a sound segment, or replay one that has finished. |

→ **Text control decisions**

### Paging or scrolling?

If the text doesn't fit on one screen, do you want users to page or scroll to see the rest? From a design point of view, paging is navigation and not hard to implement. Scrolling, on the other hand, offers a disadvantage in either aesthetics (built-in scroll bars are not very attractive) or effort (custom scroll bars require engineering). From the user's point of view, if there are just a few extra words it's easier to scroll (or for you to edit text so it fits). But if the design uses a page metaphor, users may find it more intuitive to click and advance to a new page.

### How much text?

If the text can't fit on one screen, indicate how much there is to come. Are there five screens of material, or 45? A scroll bar is both a text control and a progress indicator, since it shows in relative terms how much precedes and follows the current screen. Or pages can be num-bered—for example, "17 of 45" —so users retain a sense of where they are.

### Hyperlinks?

Hyperlinks enhance the useful-ness of interactive documents by allowing readers to jump to related topics. However, like index entries in a book, hyper-links are only useful if they lead to places that contain relevant, helpful information. Users often pursue related topics and then want to come back to where they started, so it's helpful to provide a "breadcrumb trail" back through the most recent topics visited.

### Searching?

Searching for a topic by typing or choosing a keyword is often a necessary text feature. The best way to implement searching depends on your authoring tool. Some tools include built-in search features; others don't. In some cases, having users type anything involves engineering overhead, since the product will have to cope somehow with variant spellings or mistakes; a list of key topics may be easier to design and use.

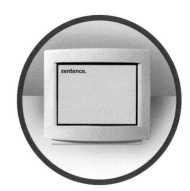

As content and functionality are integrated, what takes shape is the storyboard that will drive the rest of the project: a series of pictures and words that depict what users can see and do on every screen.

# The storyboard

**It's showtime! Not everyone's an actor, but there is an inescapable role-playing component in getting from flowchart to storyboard: the only way is to take each segment of the flowchart through a real-life walkthrough—acting out and then putting on paper all the actions and options available at every screen.**

The storyboard is a communication tool you'll use to instruct and direct everyone from illustrators to narrators to engineers. It's also a marketing tool you'll use to get buy-in from the people who need to approve, fund, and promote the project. Like the flowchart, the storyboard is a living document that's modified and updated as long as the design process continues.

Even the simplest interactive document has a set of actions that represent each screen: what the user sees when arriving there, what navigation or other controls are available, and the sequence in which events occur. The way to get all this information into one place is to block it out—to begin with the flowchart and integrate the elements of navigation, functionality, and timing.

## → Doing the walkthrough

Here's a sketch of the "Tour of Fitness Center" screen from the employee benefits manual outlined in Part One. A walkthrough allows you to design the sequence and block out what navigation controls are needed. Will the tour video start up right away, or wait for users to start it? If users want to see the tour again, will they click the video window, or a separate control on the screen?

Clicking one of the topics leads to the next screen in this scenario. What are the options here? All the topic buttons remain on the screen, so users can just click another button to change topics. Then they can click the "Go Back" arrow when they're finished with this part of the program.

## Does the narration start as soon as the image appears, or a few seconds later?

# Time is simply what keeps everything from happening at once.

Unfortunately, this does not automatically apply to interactive products. You have to help. How much you help depends on the type of product: a simple interactive document may have no timing needs at all, while a multimedia CD-ROM may have tight relationships between images, sounds, and events that take place on the screen. Part of specifying functionality and mapping it onto a storyboard is specifying *when* things happen.

As the storyboard takes shape and the interactive scenario develops, the role played by time becomes apparent: each new action you specify has a relationship in time to the preceding action. Does the narration start as soon as the image appears, or a few seconds later? How long does the screen stay black after a blackout? Every decision of this type is recorded on the storyboard at the appropriate screen.

The storyboard illustrated here is comprehensive in depicting all the options in the product, yet it's very simple because all it shows is the integration of content and functionality:

→ It does not show any stylistic elements.

→ The locations of buttons and screen elements are rough estimates.

→ It doesn't attempt to show every screen— just the ones where changes occur.

# Blocking out the action

The storyboard can be blocked out as a series of thumbnail sketches on paper or large sketches on a markerboard. At this stage capturing details is important; art skills are not. The objectives are to integrate content with controls, to begin working with real screens, and to make all the necessary decisions about functionality.

The storyboard can be taken to any level of polish, from rough sketches to color renderings that show final images. The frames of the storyboard can show every variation in content, or if that's overkill, they can show only the principal screens and indicate changes in the captions. The storyboard example at right is rough and basic, but it does the job.

What's important is winding up with a document that shows all the navigation and interaction options, so no one has to ask, "Why can't I get there from here?" or "Why can't I do that?"

The completed storyboard is the blueprint for all the design activities to come: creating the graphics and media that make up every screen.

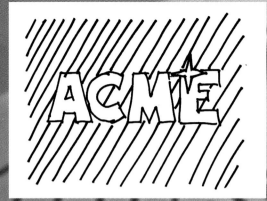

**Picture:** ACME logo fades up from black screen. Star highlight flares in corner.

Pause 5 seconds, fade to black.

**Sound:** Powerful sustained chord swells and fades.

---

# The BENEFITS of working at ACME

YOUR TIME · YOUR MONEY · YOUR HEALTH · YOUR WORK

QUIT

**Picture:** Fade up background from black. Fade in title, then each of 4 topic buttons pops on, from left to right.

**Sound:** "Welcome to Benefits" narration plays on arrival. Then silence.

**Action:** User can choose any topic or quit.

---

# YOUR TIME

- HOURS
- VACATION
- HOUDAY
- LEAVE

MENU | HELP

**Picture:** Moving to Time, Money, Health, or Work, screen pops on with subtopics listed.

**Sound:** Topic intro narration plays on arrival. Then silence.

**Action:** User can choose any subtopic, return to menu, or click Help for assistance.

---

# YOUR TIME

- HOURS
- VACATION
- HOLIDAY
- LEAVE

MENU | HELP

**Picture:** When subtopic is selected, play video from manager interview for subtopic.

**Sound:** Video soundtrack only.

**Action:** Can click video to stop or restart it. Can click a different topic at any time.

---

# YOUR TIME

- HOURS
- VACATION
- HOLIDAY
- LEAVE

MENU | HELP ◁ ▷

**Picture:** When subtopic video ends, show bullet list of key issues.

**Sound:** None.

**Action:** Can copy or paste from list, or page forward and back to additional text if necessary.

---

# YOUR TIME

- HOURS
- VACATION
- HOLIDAY
- LEAVE

MENU | HELP

**Picture:** At any time user chooses Help, current screen is dimmed and help window appears, with illustration and text.

**Sound:** Narration? TBD

**Action:** User can click return arrow when done.

storyboard
content
controls

**prototype**

Part Three

style
layout
media

## The Rules of Presentation Design

Rule #1:   Keep it simple.

Rule #2:   Keep it consistent.

Rule #3:   Know when to break the rules.

# Presentation Design

**Presentation is the style and layout of the elements on the screen. These elements are the content and controls you've defined by answering the questions "What is the product?" and "How should it work?" Part Three addresses the question "How should it look?"**

This part of the book is about the style and composition of the elements that make up an interface. No attempt is made here to teach about software tools, or to teach graphic design. Instead, the aims are to identify issues that are unique to designing with digital media, to examine each piece of an interface separately, and to set out a big-picture strategy for putting the pieces together.

The storyboard is the starting point for the presentation design process—it represents both the project's content and its controls. Most of the elements that will appear in each screen already exist in the storyboard in conceptual form. The next step is to come up with a visual language that will make these elements come to life, work together, and support the functions of each screen.

# Critical tasks of presentation design

→ Define the visual theme and style
→ Design a system of screen layouts
→ Create the structural elements of each screen (backgrounds, windows, etc.)
→ Create the control elements (buttons, etc.)
→ Integrate the media elements (images, etc.)
→ Create prototype screens

**The design tasks above represent the steps from storyboard to prototype screens. Don't be concerned that the tasks in your own process will never line up neatly and sequentially the way they do in this book. In practice, the interface design process is anything but linear.**

It's natural that you've been thinking about the product's visual appearance right from the start. You'll also be going back to revise the information and interaction design as the prototype is created. The list of critical tasks above simply breaks the process down into distinct parts, to help organize and prioritize the work.

But in one respect, the sequence of tasks does matter: big-picture decisions, such as defining an overall theme and style, have to precede any detail work, such as arranging items on individual screens or styling control elements. A unifying style can't be imposed successfully as an afterthought, once every screen is already assembled.

Users' computers, no matter how slow, will need to reproduce everything you produce.

**Pay now, or pay later.**
While you don't have to be an engineer to design prototype screens, you do have to know enough to make informed decisions about materials and methods. Just as you couldn't design a house without knowing something about how to build one, you can't design an interface without knowing some basic facts about building with digital media.

A product designed for the computer screen is reproduced electronically every time it is viewed. The images, sound, and interactivity are recreated on computers with vastly different levels of processing power and memory, possibly in a different order every time, with all kinds of interference from the computer's other programs, networks, and the circuitry that produces the picture and sound.

This is why product performance is such a big issue when building an interface. It also explains why it's essential to resist pursuing ideas for looks alone. Every aesthetic gain must be weighed against its cost in making the product more difficult to produce, and more difficult for users' computers to *reproduce*. The Survival Kit starting on the next page is a decision-maker's introduction to these issues.

*you can* Design a cool interface *without thinking about* Digital media *but when it's time to produce it* this is what you'll run into

# Digital media survival kit

**What is digital media? Everything in your product is digital media. All text, pictures, video, and sounds need to be converted to digital format to be presented on a computer.**

But there's much more to working with digital media than just converting to the digital format. Everything about creating and integrating images, sounds, and video for the computer involves unique design and production issues. Even if you're acquiring media that are already digital, such as sounds on Digital Audio Tape or images that were rendered on a computer, there are many processing issues on the way to achieving compatibility with your computer, your authoring software, and the medium on which your product will ultimately be distributed.

Volumes have been written about producing digital media. The subject is deep, technical, and could not usefully be made brief. Instead, this Survival Kit presents just the facts about digital media that directly affect design decisions.

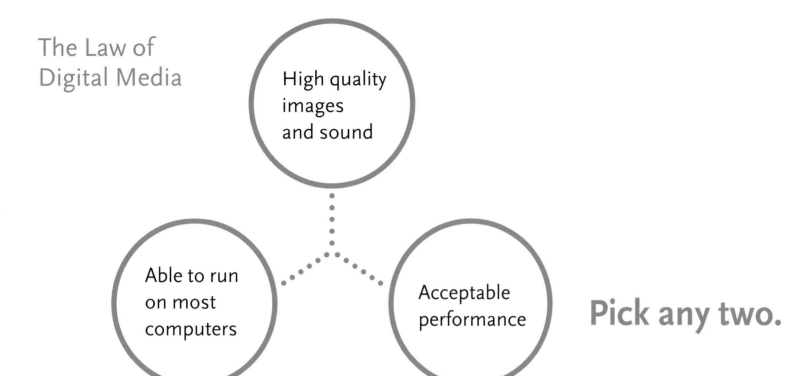

The Law of
Digital Media

High quality
images
and sound

Able to run
on most
computers

Acceptable
performance

**Pick any two.**

These basic factors need to be considered when designing for the screen:

→ the resolution of the screen

→ color and color palettes

→ compression of images and video

→ conversion of images, video, and sound to digital formats

These factors affect not only the product's quality—how good it looks and sounds—but also its behavior on user's computers:

→ its performance, or the speed of display

→ the amount of memory it needs

→ the amount of disk space it needs

→ whether it can be used at all (it must comply with the standards and capabilities of users' computers)

There are additional issues if a product is distributed on-line over a network. For example, screens must be designed for potentially slow downloading speeds, which means that images need to be compressed to lower levels of quality than might otherwise be acceptable. And because it's impossible to know what kind of equipment users have, special formatting steps are needed to make sure the images can be viewed at all.

DPI or PPI?

Readers familiar with printing processes will think of resolution in terms of DPI—dots per inch—a term that has been widely adopted by screen designers as well. But as the images on these pages show, pixels are not dots. A pixel is perfectly square, and each pixel is flush against the adjoining pixels on all four sides. And unlike the dots used to print on paper, which vary in size to produce different colors and levels of lightness, a pixel's size never changes, only its color.

# Resolution

Someone hands you a box filled with hundreds of colorful bottle caps and says, "Make these into a picture." You know the outcome will be constrained by the size, shape, and colors of the bottle caps. That awareness of your medium and its constraints is the mindset you need when designing with pixels.

**Primary constraint: screen resolution**

Most computer graphics tools were designed to produce images for printing, so the resolution of the images they generate is limited only by the resolution of the printer. But no matter what these graphics tools are capable of, the resolution of images viewed on the computer screen is limited by the screen's resolution—typically 72 or 96 dots per inch, which is similar to the coarse graininess of newspaper photos.

**How does resolution influence your design?**

→ Images appear to have jagged edges. You'll need to take measures to avoid this, both when you produce design elements and when you assemble or layer them together.

→ Images can't show a high level of detail at 72 dots per inch. Design elements such as mechanical objects need to be greatly enlarged to show fine details.

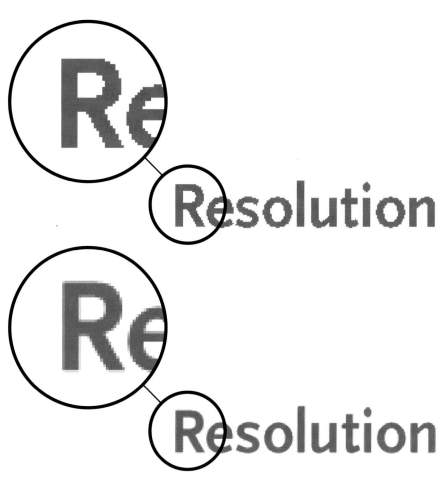

Resolution

Resolution

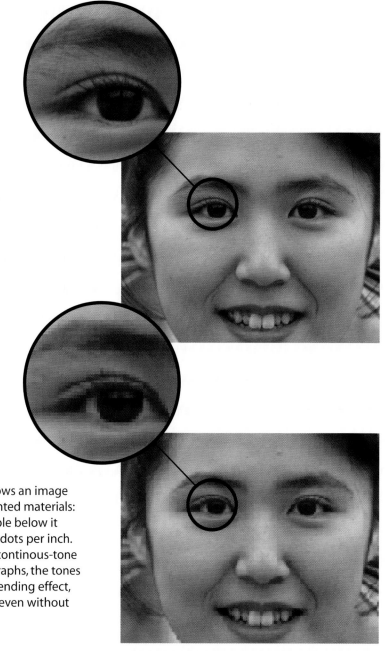

The top example above shows how curves and diagonals appear jagged when represented by the pixels on a computer screen. The example below it shows the result of "anti-aliasing," a technique that changes the pixel colors along the edge of an object to create a smoother-looking curve or diagonal. (There's more about anti-aliasing on page 70, and a look at anti-aliased text on page 108.)

The example above right shows an image at a typical resolution for printed materials: 300 dots per inch. The example below it shows the same image at 72 dots per inch.

Note that within a single continous-tone image such as these photographs, the tones of color produce a natural blending effect, so curved lines look smooth even without anti-aliasing.

Anti-aliasing blends the edge colors of an object with the colors of its background, to smooth out the jagged edges produced by the screen's low resolution.

This example shows a solid black image over solid green without anti-aliasing, then with anti-aliasing, and finally with all the solid black and green removed to show the pixels that were partially blended.

 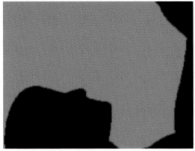 

# Anti-aliasing

**Elements on an interactive screen are much like actors on a stage—they are frequently brought on or taken off, or moved around. That's why they need to be created as independent objects. But when one of these objects is placed in front of another, a clearly visible "aliased" edge sets it apart.**

How anti-aliasing is applied to an object depends on how the object is produced. If it's a computer-rendered image, the rendering software can often anti-alias the edges against the background as the object is being created.

If it's a scanned object, the original background has to be removed from the scanned image, which may require substantial manual retouching. Then the anti-aliasing may be done by composing the object together with

its new background and blending its edges using the imaging software.

Anti-aliasing can be both a blessing and a curse. By blending the edge colors of an object with the colors of its background, anti-aliasing creates a fringe of color that becomes visible when the object is placed over any *other* background. This means that you need to create a custom version of the object for each of its anticipated backgrounds, as shown at right.

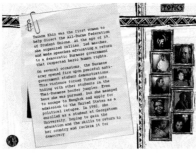

In these images, the paper clip was created as a separate element because the letter and photograph change positions from front to back when clicked, and the clip always needs to remain the frontmost item.

The closeups at right show how the paper clips appear in the two screens above.

When shown without their respective backgrounds, the customized edges for each paper clip are visible.

To dramatize the effects of anti-aliasing, the clips have been reversed. It becomes evident why objects need retouching when placed over different backgrounds.

"Full color" requires 24 bits of memory for each pixel, which can produce over 16 million colors. But for most interactive products, color is limited to 8 bits per pixel, or 256 colors. Here is a palette of 256 colors. It's easy to see why it might not do justice to a full-color photograph.

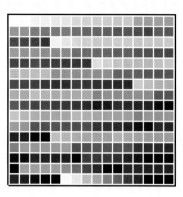

# Color and palettes

**If you've shopped for a computer or been around computer artists, you've heard talk about the "number of colors" or "color depth." Color depth determines whether your design can contain just a few hundred colors, or a few million.**

Color depth simply means the number of bits of information used to describe each pixel in an image. For example, an image in which 24 bits of data are used to describe each pixel is said to have 24-bit color depth. An image with a high color depth uses up a lot of memory, but it can contain a large number of colors. If only eight bits are available to describe each pixel, the image is limited to a much smaller pool of colors than if 16 or 24 bits are available.

In 1995 the vast majority of personal computers in homes and businesses had video hardware capable of displaying only 8-bit images, or 256 colors at once. For an interactive product to look good on these computers, every image in the product must be converted to use a palette of 256 colors. If this isn't done, the computer still displays only 256 colors out of the thousands in the original image, and the result can be far from acceptable.

The two pictures at left were digitized and stored using full 24-bit color. That means these pictures require 24 bits of memory for each pixel, and can be composed from a palette of up to 16.7 million colors.

The new versions at left have been reduced to 8-bit color depth, each separately with its own palette of 256 colors. Since each image's palette is customized to use the colors most needed in that image, these pictures look pretty good.

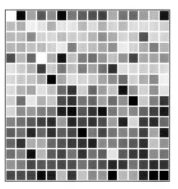
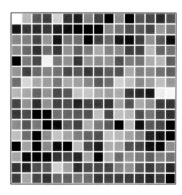

The trouble with 8-bit images begins when you need to have more than one image on the screen at the same time (which is often). The computer can use only one palette at any given time, but as you can see from the palettes for these two images, there can be vast differences in the colors they include.

**The basic tasks of managing color**

| What | Why | How |
|------|-----|-----|
| **Reduce color depth (to 256 colors)** | To avoid running up against the limitations of users' hardware. | A straightforward process of indicating the desired color depth. This feature is available in most image-processing tools, such as Adobe Photoshop, and in some authoring tools, such as Macromedia Director. The feature is usually called "Indexing" or "Remapping." |
| **Choose a palette** | To indicate *which* 256 colors should be used when the color depth is reduced—when all the colors in the image are mapped to just 256 colors. | Applications used to reduce color depth provide a selection mechanism from which to choose a palette—either the system palette, which is the computer's default palette, or any palette that has been previously saved. |
| **Create a custom palette for an image** | To produce the best possible colors for an image. | Image-processing applications provide the option to create a custom palette when reducing color depth, using a palette that best preserves the colors of the original image, rather than any existing palette. This custom palette is saved with the image and used whenever the image is displayed. |
| **Create one palette for several images** | To avoid having images with conflicting palettes sharing the screen. | Some image-processing tools, such as DeBabelizer from Equilibrium, include a batch processing mode that produces a single palette containing the best possible colors for a group of images. |

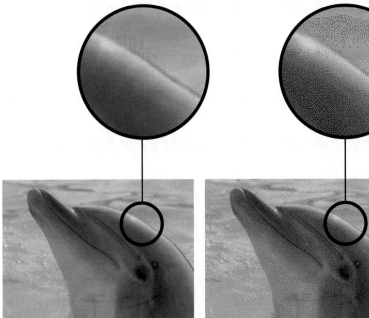

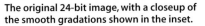

The original 24-bit image, with a closeup of the smooth gradations shown in the inset.

Reduction to 8-bit color with dithering, but without a custom palette. The closeup shows the banding effect that results.

Reduction to 8-bit color with dithering and a custom palette.

Reduction to 8-bit color without dithering or a custom palette.

# dither

**n: A state of indecision**
**v: To be nervously irresolute**

Dithering is the single most valuable processing technique that can be applied to images whose color depth is reduced.

→ It simulates the colors from the original image that are not available in the new, reduced palette.

→ It creates smooth, natural-looking gradations between adjacent colors, rather than the sharp divisions that can result from palette reduction.

Most image-processing tools have a dithering option that can be applied as part of reducing color depth. To simulate colors that are not available in the palette, dithering combines pixels of complementary colors into a diffusion pattern. Since the new color is created by a dot pattern rather than by blending, the result is visibly grainy, as shown in the example above. However, even a grainy 8-bit image is preferable to an undithered one, since dithering infinitely extends the range of available colors.

Without compression, a 4" x 3" video image would require your computer to process about 50 million bits of information each second. Let's say this is no problem for your processor. It's still twenty times the data that a double-speed CD-ROM drive could move from the disc in a second. And that's just the image. What if you wanted sound, too?

# Compression is your friend

**Designing for the screen means having to deal with compression. There's no way around it. The pictures you want to display—both still and video—need to be compressed so they can be stored, processed, and moved around the computer fast enough to produce good interactive performance.**

Topics like compression can sound at first like engineering work—not the sort of thing you signed up for as designer. But what if, for example, your design relied on a sequence of large images for a particularly powerful impact? You'd be disappointed to learn at the last minute that users would see these images at a fraction of the speed you were counting on. It's to avoid such surprises that there should be a touch of engineer in every interface designer.

But why can't a computer display images as fast as a TV using forty-year-old technology? That's like asking why human babies take a year to walk when ponies can do it in a day. The computer processes each bit of information in the image through a sophisticated central "brain." Your TV doesn't save the images it displays. It doesn't need to search for them on a disk or process them in any way—it just paints a continuous stream of color onto the screen.

## The digital video quality tradeoff

The higher the image quality, the lower the playback quality. A better-looking video image requires more data about each frame and more frames per second. But the rate at which data can be transferred from a disk is limited, and when that limit is reached, the video begins to have skips and gaps.

To illustrate this tradeoff, here are sample frames compressed at two different *frame rates* (number of frames per second), keeping a constant *data rate* (the amount of data transferred per second). The first image looks better because when fewer frames are displayed per second, each can contain more image data.

**15 fps**

**30 fps**

For both still images and video, the object of compression is to speed up processing time and reduce the amount of storage space needed.

An uncompressed, full-screen image is made up of millions of bits of information (640 x 480 pixels at 24 bits per pixel). It takes a lot of processing time to read that much data from a disk and display it on the screen. Compression software can reduce the size of an image file by 90% or more, with little or no loss of quality.

The need to reduce processing time is greatest for digital video, because as many as 30 images are displayed each second.

As an example, a modest-sized video image of 240 x 180 pixels would need to play at a rate of nearly 4000 Kbytes per second without compression. On commercial CD-ROMs, video images of that size are typically compressed to 200 Kbytes per second or less, a saving of 95%.

# Compression: how and when

**In still images:** Beyond reducing color depth, image-processing programs let you apply a variety of compression methods that make the image file smaller still. Compressing a file is typically done by a simple command to the imaging software, but there are many compressors to choose from.

→ "Lossless" compressors reduce file size without altering the image quality.

→ "Lossy" compressors reduce file size by eliminating some of the image data, which does affect quality. You'll need to experiment to find the right level of compression.

There's no need to become an expert on compressors. Their documentation should tell you which compressor will do the job you need.

**In digital video:** Compression is usually applied as a separate step after digitizing the original video. Although digitizing video is a specialized process beyond the scope of this book, designers need to consider the effects of video compression:

→ There's an inversely proportional relationship between image quality and playback quality, as shown in the adjoining example.

→ Decisions about the size of the video image and the combination of video with other media elements will significantly influence the playback performance of the product.

Unless the video is already digitized, plan to hire a specialist to digitize and compress it.

# Laws of survival

**No matter what the medium—video, sound, or images—high quality means lots of data, and makes enormous demands on the power and memory of users' computers. The goal is to find the balance point where both performance and quality are least compromised.**

To a computer, all media are alike. They are all made up of bits of information, which can be moved from disk to processor to screen only so fast and only so many bits at a time. Producing a responsive, smooth-running product means compromising quality just enough to obtain good performance on users' computers. How good is good enough? Users will expect an art gallery on CD-ROM to meet much higher visual standards than a home page on the Internet.

But aren't computer speeds doubling each year, and network speeds even faster than that? They are, but the data-richness of media is growing right in step. Eight-bit images will give way to higher densities, video will become navigable 3-D reality—and the fast-growing number of users on public networks is already slowing traffic to a crawl. It's safe to expect that designers will have to continue balancing quality and performance well into the next century.

# Always...

## Buy high, sell low

Digitize images, video, and sound at the highest possible resolution, and reduce it later. Digitizing at low resolution saves on memory and storage up front (which can be tempting when you know the final product will have low resolution anyway), but the resulting media contain relatively little information. This makes retouching and editing operations more difficult and less effective.

## Save the best for last

Reduce the resolution of the content last, after you've finished all other processing operations. For example, anti-aliasing can't be applied once color depth has been reduced, because there aren't enough colors left to produce the smooth gradations needed for an anti-aliased edge.

## Keep an audit trail

Keep a written record of every process used on an image, video, or sound file. For an image file, for example, note any changes in size, color, lightness, and settings used to create special imaging effects. That way, when you achieve the perfect effect and need to reproduce it on another image, you won't have to say, "Now, how'd I do that?"

## Protect the crown jewels

Keep an original high-resolution copy of every media file you use. These take up lots of space so you'll need a good archiving setup, but without them you may be unable to make any necessary changes in future versions of the same image, video, or sound material.

# Then...

When content has been processed and tweaked to perfection, move it to a different computer and get ready for a shock. Variances in colors and brightness from one monitor to another can be dramatic, and the performance of video, sound, and animation may be entirely different on the new computer. The best strategy is to test on many playback platforms, to avoid subtleties in design that may be hard to reproduce, and to design media for the lowest-common-denominator computers on which the product may be used.

# Setting the style

**Style is no more than the sum of the characteristics you can perceive about an object, a person, or an experience. But setting a style becomes complex when different types of media, each with its own style, are brought together into a shared environment.**

A style is not inherently good or bad, though it can be pleasant or unpleasant. What makes it pleasant is often whether attention was paid to creating a style in the first place—to assembling a unified set of elements that work together to produce a cohesive personality.

This means that to create a style that works for an interface, it's more important to be a thoughtful integrator of stylistic elements than a skilled artist.

How people evaluate a style is probably most influenced by society: the social standards of "appropriate" likes and dislikes that people acquire in early childhood and update as fashions change throughout their lives.

It follows that choosing a style for an interactive project begins by establishing what style users will find consistent with the ideas represented by the content.

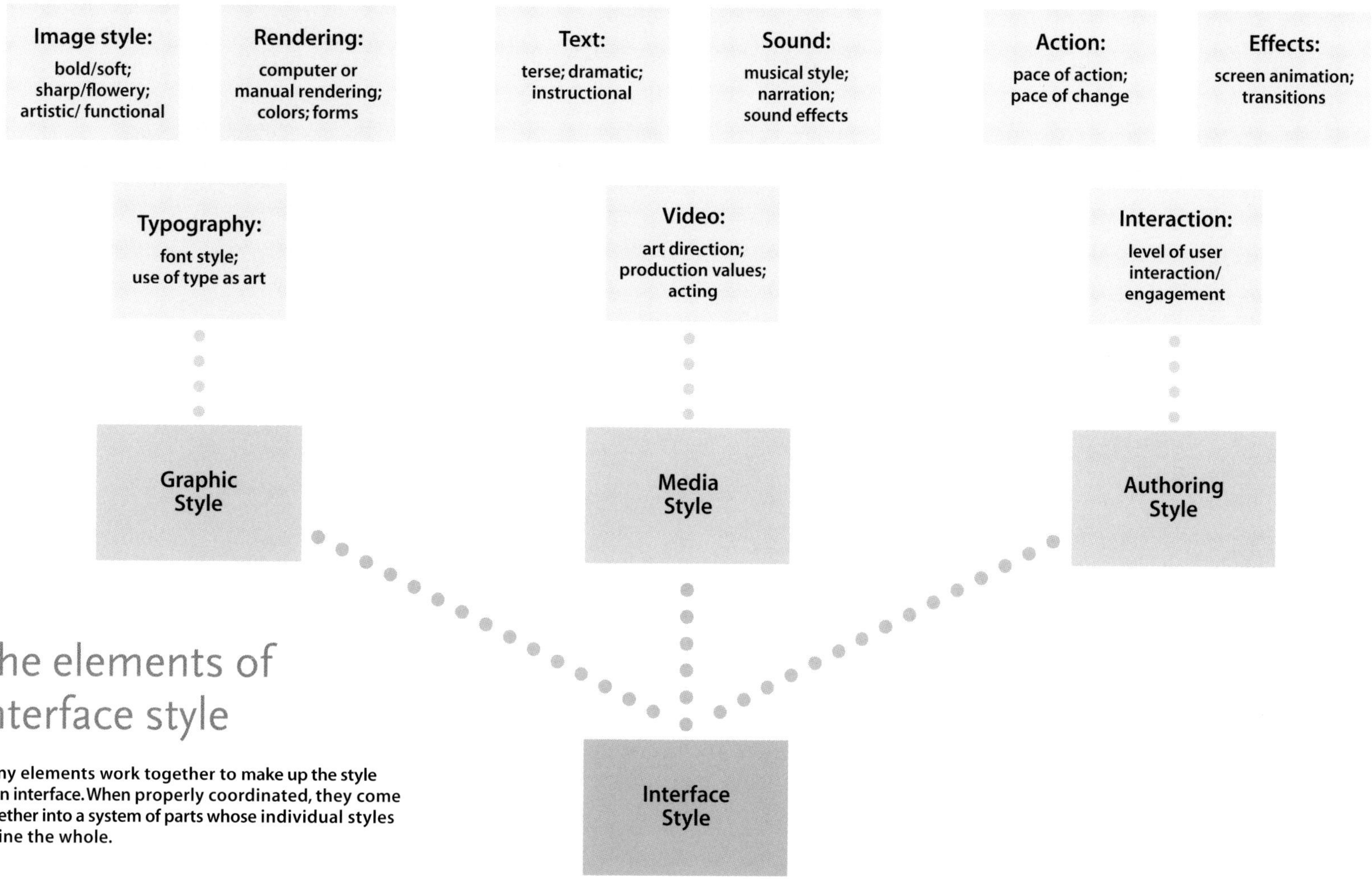

**Image style:**
bold/soft;
sharp/flowery;
artistic/ functional

**Rendering:**
computer or
manual rendering;
colors; forms

**Text:**
terse; dramatic;
instructional

**Sound:**
musical style;
narration;
sound effects

**Action:**
pace of action;
pace of change

**Effects:**
screen animation;
transitions

**Typography:**
font style;
use of type as art

**Video:**
art direction;
production values;
acting

**Interaction:**
level of user
interaction/
engagement

**Graphic
Style**

**Media
Style**

**Authoring
Style**

# The elements of interface style

**Many elements work together to make up the style
of an interface. When properly coordinated, they come
together into a system of parts whose individual styles
define the whole.**

**Interface
Style**

Because this product is a reference source for young children, it relies on bright colors, a cartoon-like rendering style, and images designed to appeal to the interests of its audience.

# How content defines style

What is the single most powerful impression produced by your content? Is it a message of corporate identity? A sense of history and culture? Of a time or a place? If you can identify the quality or characteristic that lends substance to your project, you've begun to define its style.

The elements in the chart on the previous page—music and art, writing and typography—represent only the visual or observable part of an interface's style. But the underlying meaning and identity of the style come from the content itself, and are not observable but conceptual. You can think of this conceptual aspect of the style as the theme or personality that best represents the material.

Themes can derive from many contexts and topics: an era, a location, an ethnic heritage, nature, technology, finance, and so on. As the examples here show, a coherent style results from defining a theme first, and then making every design element consistent with that theme. This applies not only to images but to all the elements that make up the sights and sounds of the experience.

The style of this interactive employee benefits manual can be described as modern, businesslike, international—with enough fun in it (the piggy bank icon, the lively colors) to keep it from being boring. This style is a good match for the content, and is consistent with the image the company wants to project.

This interactive catalog of arts information has the same purpose as the benefits manual above: to direct people to facts in a limited database. However, the influence of the content on this catalog's style is evident in its colors, images, and typography: it's an expression of creativity rather than business.

These four images, collected for a bicycle club's home page, have nothing in common stylistically. They're good raw material because they have simple subjects that are universally easy to understand, and they are visually interesting and dynamic. The problem in combining them into a single screen is that they are worlds apart in colors, rendering styles, backgrounds, and more.

# Stylistic unity

**Choosing a style and making it work for all the diverse content in a project is like furnishing a new apartment. You'd like every piece in the living room to be a perfect match, but in reality all you need is the right rug to make the pieces you have work together.**

Obtaining good visual content is hard enough without imposing stylistic constraints on it. If you have the resources to create new images, you can specify their style down to the last detail. But if you're searching for images from your corporate database, or from inexpensive public sources, the main requirement is that they should be interesting and a good fit for the information they represent.

Making dissimilar images work together usually involves looking beyond their individual styles to a meta-style for the entire group. A meta-style is the project's overall style—the one that's driven by the project's goals and personality, whether it's a businesslike benefits manual, an elegant arts catalog, or a fun-loving bicycle club home page.

In this example, the greatest obstacles to stylistic unity were the backgrounds and colors of the original images. (This is a very common problem.) The screen at right shows how the images are integrated and made to work together by removing their backgrounds and altering their tones to fit within a particular color family. Once this is done, the dynamic relationships among the images can be balanced by adjusting their sizes and angles.

# The goal is unity, not uniformity.

The appearance of a screen depends on two things:

→ the styles of pre-existing content elements, such as photos and illustrations

→ the designer's style decisions, including color, illustration techniques, and so on

If the first is allowed to drive the second, the design process becomes reactive and less likely to succeed in pulling all the individual styles together.

Diversity in content may be a design challenge, but it's rarely bad for the end product. If every image were created in the same style, the result would be monotonous no matter how good the images looked. Variety can produce much more interesting results.

Since the goal is stylistic unity, not uniformity, the designer's role is to create a harmonious environment in which disparate elements can coexist. A design that can accommodate diversity really pays off when content changes occur at the last minute, or when projects are updated with new content.

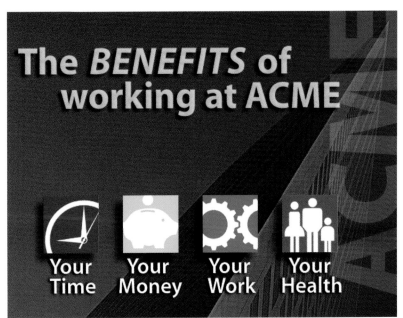

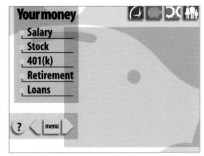

# Interface families

**Few interface problems are solved by designing a single screen or a number of independent screens. What often works best is a system of visual and structural elements that form the basis for a family of related screens.**

Elements in an interface family must work both as a group and as independent pieces. Here are a few examples:

→ distinct images in a montage on the main screen, used individually in topic screens

→ distinct colors in the main screen, used individually as key colors in topic screens

→ a hierarchical family of images, such as a clock and clock parts, or a tree and leaves

As these elements are repeated from screen to screen, they are kept interesting by variations in their sizes, angles, colors, regions of detail, and so on. Parent-child relationships among the elements can be used to represent the hierarchical relationships among screens.

In addition to the visual elements in the family, functional elements such as buttons, menu styles, and navigation options are also shared and repeated among screens.

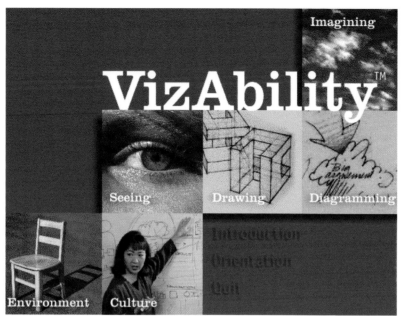

The interface families shown here illustrate how continuity can be achieved in both appearance and message by creating a hierarchical system of images. In both examples, the main navigational screen is an image whose most significant parts represent the main topic areas. The individual topic screens are derived from the images in their main screens.

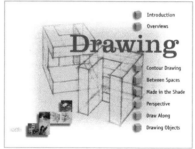

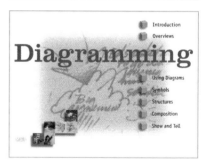

Artistic composition has two elements:

1. The composition of the whole picture.
2. The creation of the various forms which, by standing in different relationships to each other, decide the composition of the whole. —Kandinsky

# Layout

**Like all aspects of interface design, screen layout has a functional side as well as a visual one. How you arrange objects on the screen determines not only how good they look but how easy they are to understand and to use.**

Objects on the screen may serve a variety of different purposes besides being part of a visual arrangement:

→ Some are structural, such as windows and borders that delineate regions for content.

→ Some are informational, such as the words and pictures that deliver the content.

→ Some are functional, such as the buttons and other controls for interaction.

In fact, an interface may contain no elements at all whose purpose is strictly visual. It's clear then why arranging elements on the screen has more than visual consequences: it can make content elements communicate more or less clearly, and control elements easier or harder to use.

The facing page shows the evolution in the layout of a single screen, illustrating how its components can be manipulated and arranged to work together more effectively.

This layout begins life as an image map. A set of large icons have been created to represent the main topics of an interactive product. However, because these images are boxed into squares, they give the image map a stiff appearance.

Without changing the sizes or positions of the images, the screen can be made dramatically more fluid by removing the boundaries between items. But the equal sizes of the items and their geometric alignment keep the layout static.

To break up the symmetry and add dynamic tension among the images, they are resized, rotated, and moved into positions that complement each other's shapes—in effect, moved around through trial and error until they "fit" like a puzzle. Another approach might be to create subtle overlaps, to add the illusion of depth.

Because the unequal sizes of items in the image map distorted the relative imporance of the five topics, a new approach is attempted in which the images are used as actual icons. This creates a more elegant and quiet look than the full-screen activity, but results in a very monotonous background.

To revive the screen dynamics, the background is changed to a contrasting tone and the title is enlarged to a much more prominent size.

Finally, the image map is brought back into the background. These images no longer serve as hot (clickable) items, but they complement their more pronounced icon counterparts.

After 100 years of evolution in automobile interfaces, you can get into any car and know where to find the steering wheel, the clutch, the brakes, and the gas pedal.

# Layout conventions

**People look at the screens in an interactive product with many expectations from the world of printed pages. Taking these expectations into account results in a more usable interface, even if the design looks nothing like a page.**

Certain layout conventions based on print documents can be useful in interactive products because they help people concentrate on the content, instead of on how to work the machinery that takes them there. It isn't necessary to use print conventions in screen design, just to recognize their existence so you can help viewers stay oriented and avoid sending them unintentional messages.

For example, users of Western languages are conditioned to

→ scan from top left to bottom right

→ assume that larger items are more significant

→ assume that items "above" have primacy over items "below"

→ look for "more to come" signals at the bottom center or right

# What's wrong with these screens?

The designer may just have been aiming to balance background colors or head angles on the screen, but users may infer from the photo positions that the men are higher-ranking or more important than the women.

The wording of these items says clearly that one topic precedes the other, but their placement sends a mixed message about which should be viewed first.

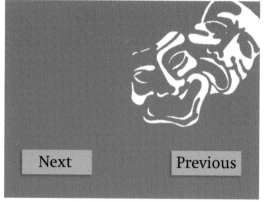

Basketball players might think this screen is fine, while golfers… The disproportionate sizes of the items are true to life, but suggest an unintended scale of importance.

These buttons are clearly marked, but their positions are the opposite of what users would expect. People would probably click in the wrong place several times before being retrained for these counter-intuitive locations.

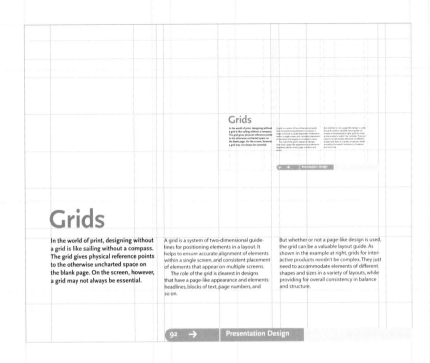

# Grids

**In the world of print, designing without a grid is like sailing without a compass. The grid gives physical reference points to the otherwise uncharted space on the blank page. On the screen, however, a grid may not always be essential.**

A grid is a system of two-dimensional guidelines for positioning elements in a layout. It helps to ensure accurate alignment of elements within a single screen, and consistent placement of elements that appear on multiple screens.

The role of the grid is clearest in designs that have a page-like appearance and elements: headlines, blocks of text, page numbers, and so on.

But whether or not a page-like design is used, the grid can be a valuable layout guide. As shown in the example at right, grids for interactive products needn't be complex. They just need to accommodate elements of different shapes and sizes in a variety of layouts, while providing for overall consistency in balance and structure.

## Interactive exercise

Look at the word "Prototyping" in the lower-right corner of this page. Then lift the page to look at the same word on the page directly below it. Are the words in the exact same location? Could you tell if they weren't perfectly aligned? No– because this is a book! But on the screen there is no page to turn; the new screen pops into place on top of the old one, and any item that's not aligned jumps visibly.

The solution to this problem is called registration. It means making sure an element that appears on multiple screens *doesn't* jump, by aligning it to the same reference point on every screen.

These two screens are identical; the lower one shows the guidelines used for alignment. This design doesn't use a page-style layout, yet it's evident that it benefits from the use of a grid, particularly because it's based on geometric regions of the screen. Note that using a grid doesn't have to create any rigidity or any particular symmetry in the layout. It merely adds subtle alignment and a sense of balance.

# Designs without grids

Many designs for the screen make no attempt to mimic the printed page. They may have more in common with a cinematic screen or theatrical stage, a billboard, or a comic book, or they may bear no resemblance at all to existing media. In such products, the designer may intentionally choose not to use a grid.

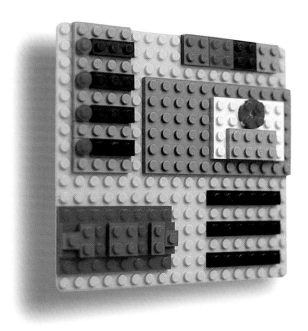

# Interface elements

**A good interface is a construction kit: a set of elements that fit together like building blocks, and can be moved and reused in many different combinations. When these elements are assembled into a family of screens, they work together to produce a coherent interface.**

Up to this point, it's been important to look at the style and layout of an interface as a unified system. But while the system has to be conceived as a whole, it can only be created in parts. As the interface is assembled, its parts are used in a variety of screens, in different sizes, colors, and positions. These elements work as the building blocks of the interface, and their family relationship produces a sense of continuity and consistency.

In the upcoming pages, this system is deconstructed into its basic elements, focusing on each element in turn to identify

→ the role that the element plays in an interface

→ specific issues the element can raise for design, production, and usability

→ interesting examples and types of uses

# What is an interface made of?

## Background

The backdrop that sets the scene, whether realistic or abstract, decorative or fully integrated with the content.

## Windows and panels

Screen areas, with or without frames or borders, that contain media or delineate different functional regions.

## Images

Photographs or illustrations that may be part of the content, graphic design, or both.

## Video

Digital movies of live action or animation, often with a soundtrack.

## Buttons and controls

Pictures, labels, and other devices that represent topics to visit or tools to control things.

## Text

Any words on the screen, from headings and labels to entire documents.

## Sound

Music, narration, and sound effects that deliver content, reinforce action, and contribute to overall style.

## Animation

Any motion created using the authoring tool (not as digitized video), from moving text to screen transitions and special effects.

These examples show that a background can be made interesting by creating areas of emphasis, rather than filling the entire screen or providing uniform coverage.

# Backgrounds

**Although every element on the screen contributes to the look and feel of the interface, the background carries the greatest load simply because it fills so much of the screen. Like the backdrop in a theater, it provides the location and context for all the action on the stage.**

The background does not, of course, have to play a dominant role in the design. In many cases a purely decorative or plain background is all that's needed. But even in a passive role, the background serves two critical purposes:

→ It influences the look, balance, and location of all other elements on the screen.

→ It fills the empty space so other elements are not floating objects.

No matter how tightly a background is integrated with other screen elements, it usually needs to be created as an independent image so those elements can move and change in front of it. This means that to make the background really work in the interface, it has to be composed together with the other elements that will appear on top of it, to make sure all objects are distinct and to adjust colors or contrast where necessary.

# Shopping for wallpaper?

The wealth of available images—stock photos of every style and subject, scanned artwork, textures—makes choosing a background seem as easy as selecting wallpaper (and much easier to apply). But a background works only if it's an integral part of the design, and not just chosen as an independent image.

The background at top left reinforces other elements in the interface, such as the quiet colors and bold, angular graphics, and it repeats the image of the button for the active topic.

The two screens beside it are much less successful. Although the photos selected as backgrounds are striking, they have no stylistic relationship to anything else on the screen.

A background can be strong when its role is to make a design statement, and toned down when it needs to make way for other elements.

**Anything can be a window**

Windows can take many forms. It may suit the design to display content in a picture frame, through the eyepiece of a microscope, or on a television or computer screen.

# Windows and panels

**A window or panel can be any distinct region of the screen. Windows are usually set aside to hold media, while panels may simply enhance the structural features of the design, or add depth or color.**

There's no reason to think of a window in your design as anything resembling the windows that contain documents in your computer's application programs.

Frames and borders around windows are useful only when they serve an integral purpose in the design. For most purposes, text, images, and video work best when integrated with their surrounding images, or set off in a clear area, free of unnecessary boxes or frames.

Windows and structural panels present a wide range of screen design solutions:

→ They delineate a region of the screen for a particular purpose or type of content.

→ They anchor design elements within the structure so they don't appear to float.

→ They help to integrate media into the surrounding environment.

## Distinct content regions

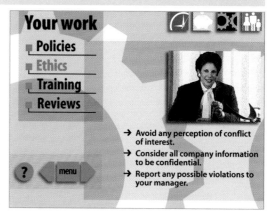

In this screen, the title, list of topics, and buttons float in the layout, and it isn't clear where content will align in the large, empty area.

Panels of translucent color create anchors for the floating elements, giving them structure and alignment without hiding the background.

The panels delineate the topics list, buttons, and content area to give the viewer a sense of the distinct functional regions at a glance.

## Competing elements

It's impossible to read the title of this screen, and there is no portion of the screen where the title could be moved to improve matters.

A panel behind the title helps the words to pop out and solves the problem of competing elements, but produces a stiff, hard-edged contrast to the flowing illustration.

By using a translucent panel with soft edges, the words become visible but the background is allowed to show through, producing an unbroken, natural-looking image.

Answer

Sometimes a button works best as a part of the imagery on the screen. It can be any sort of picture that represents the button's function or the content it leads to. The look of the button should come from the style of the interface.

Other times a button works best when it's completely unadorned. For example, the choices presented in an instructional exercise need to be styled plainly to avoid competing with the content. But simplicity itself is a design choice: it should support the goals of the screen as a whole.

# Buttons and other controls

**Buttons and controls are the tangible parts of the interface, the objects users interact with. Naturally they need to be clear and unambiguous, but that doesn't have to mean predictable or dull. Controls are an opportunity to involve users in the content, and to intrigue, amuse, and entertain them.**

What makes a good button or control?

→ A control can be any part of a screen or region of an image. It doesn't need to look like a button or be a discrete object.

→ A control has to reveal its purpose at first glance. If that's not possible with a picture alone, use words.

→ Controls need to match the style and composition of the screen. They don't need to be designed as a separate grouping or control panel.

→ A control should be proportional in importance to the function it represents. Putting an Exit sign over a door makes a clever way to quit, but not a very usable one if it's lost in the background graphics.

# Controls as integral design elements

Everything on this screen is a button, except the background and borders. The photograph and underlying letter both act as buttons whose function is to bring the clicked item to the top; the globe brings political information to the screen; the small pictures at right lead to stories about other people; and the Topics button leads back to the main menu.

The AppleCD Audio Player in Macintosh system software is a set of buttons designed to look... just like buttons. While this kind of "control panel" appearance can lend a cold style to an information product, it works perfectly here because the desired look is, in fact, an electronic control panel.

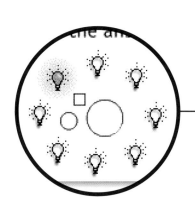

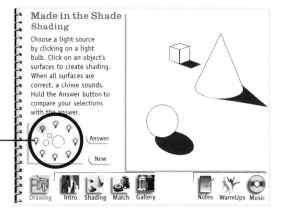

The controls shown in the inset can be used to explore several different physical scenarios. By clicking a different light bulb, users can change the position of the light source to observe the effect on the shapes of shadows. The light bulbs in this interface both represent the light source and simulate its effects.

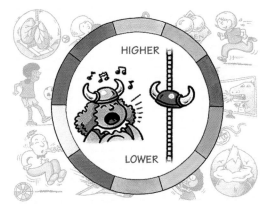

This example shows a slider used to change the pitch of the opera singer's voice. Although this slider makes no attempt to look like a typical interface control, its purpose is obvious from its context in the program and its clear labeling.

# Breaking the rules

Consistent positioning is important when laying out controls that appear on multiple screens. But complete and unvarying consistency can make for boring layouts. When is it safe to break the rules and vary the positions of controls?

**Not OK**

→ If a screen contains many controls, users can easily get confused if these aren't always in the same location.

→ If the same control is used very frequently, users need to find it in the same place every time.

→ If several controls have a similar look or function, such as video controls marked with symbols, their positions relative to each other should never change.

**OK**

When there are few controls on the screen, and they are easy to distinguish from their surroundings and from each other, it's often possible to change their placement without affecting ease of use. The two screens at right are from the same product and contain the same controls. The different locations of the controls in each screen aren't likely to cause confusion, especially since they are presented in a similar way in both layouts.

# Laying out controls

There is no one right place to put buttons or controls on the screen. What matters is ease of access and ease of recognition.

It often makes sense to group controls together in one location, both for easier access and to reserve screen real estate for other content. But grouping many buttons together can result in a cluttered look and feel.

One way to avoid this problem on screens with many controls is to group them by function rather than putting them all together in one place. For example, navigation controls can be grouped in one cluster and topic controls in another. Clustering makes it easier to style the groups differently, which can help users recognize them as well as make the design more interesting.

Through popular usage, these icons have become instantly recognizable. They could be used in an appropriate context—such as a travel kiosk at an airport—to request a bus schedule and reserve a non-smoking room in a hotel.

But icons don't have to look like pictures in airport terminals. What's important is that people should be able to interpret them instantly. It's up to the designer to make sure that the screen makes the purpose of the icons obvious, so users won't have to wonder what the pictures mean.

# Icons

Icon-based interfaces have become the standard on nearly all computers, and the term "icon" is often used to refer to any clickable picture on the screen. But a true icon is not just a picture. It is a special class of button that symbolically depicts what it does.

An icon can be clearly understood to stand for something—if it's a good icon, always the *same* thing. A question mark has a universal meaning across languages and cultures, in any medium, in any context. A light bulb, on the other hand, may mean inspiration or ideas, or light in the literal sense.

A good icon is:

→ Instantly recognizable. Its meaning is obvious at a glance.

→ International. Its meaning is cross-cultural (think of the symbols on restroom doors).

→ Scalable. It works equally well in a wide range of sizes.

→ Simple. Simple, solid shapes may work better than detailed pictures with fine lines.

## Component images

Like most designs, this navigation screen began as a single integrated vision. But if it were created as a standalone image, its small topic images would be hard to work with. They need to be reused in topic screens and for other purposes such as creating a highlight effect when users click them. For these reasons, the elements will be created as separate objects and composed together on the screen.

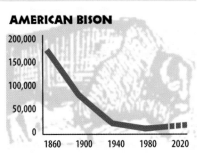

# Images

**Interfaces contain two kinds of images:** *standalone images*, **such as a photo of an executive above a block of text in an annual report, and** *component images* **that are part of a scene, such as a map with buildings and people, composed into an information montage.**

Standalone images originate as individual pictures, so placing or moving them in the interface is relatively easy. Component images have more demanding requirements: they are designed as part of a composed screen, but often need to work as separate elements, too. For example, items placed on a map may need to move or disappear in a different view of the same map.

This means that whatever the source of the images, whether they're created on the computer or scanned from original art, they will be much easier to work with if every component is created separately.

### Shadows

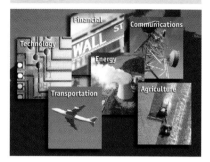

In many cases, a simple shadow can make an image appear to be better integrated with its surroundings. This easy technique can make a big visual difference with little effort.

### Vignetted edges

If you aren't creating a database of hundreds of images, it may be worth the effort to vignette an image by removing its background. This results in an elegant image that can integrate seamlessly with other content, and support a wide variety of styles.

### Soft or irregular edges

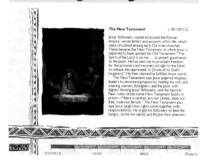

On the screen, images can be any shape you like. Image-processing programs can easily render soft or irregular edges, or blend them into the background. Or an image could be cropped into a wedge, a star, or any shape the design calls for.

# Integrating images

An interface might include images of all types—scanned photos, cartoons, computer-rendered three-dimensional objects, and so on. There are no right or wrong types to use. What matters is how an image becomes part of an interface. It's easier to control how images are integrated into the design than how they're created in the first place. And controlling the integration method is an effective way to maintain a unified style.

The idea is to look beyond the image's original shape and style to determine what integration treatment best supports the design. Snapshots in a photo album, for example, have nice sharp edges and square corners, and there are times when a sharp square snapshot is just what an interface needs. At other times that treatment might be inappropriate, or boring.

The screens on this page illustrate a few ways to integrate scanned images.

## "How would I want the text to look if the authoring tool weren't a factor?"

Multimedia authoring tools are sophisticated screen composition tools, but they are not precision typography tools. They can compose text that's seamlessly integrated with other interface elements, but the text elements themselves may be limited in style and format. For the greatest flexibility and control of formats, spacing, and special effects, text can be created separately using specialized tools, and then integrated using the authoring tool.

No multimedia authoring tool could produce the curved alphabet in this index screen, so it was set on a curve in Adobe Illustrator, saved as a bitmapped image, and then composed into the interface.

# Text

**All the elements in an interface play a role in design. But while some may be purely aesthetic and have no role in the content, text is always content. Even when words are used decoratively as part of a background or image, their meaning matters.**

Text on the screen serves many masters: it has to look right for the message; it has to be easy to read; and it also has to work in the interface. Fitting the look of the type to the message is what typographic design is all about: choosing the appropriate typeface from the thousands available, and getting the size, spacing, color, and format just right. But these are the issues of typography in any medium; they aren't unique to integrating text into an interface.

What does it take to make text work on the screen? Among other things, it requires a balancing act between design goals and reasonable effort. The effort is needed to compensate for the limited formatting available in most authoring tools, the low resolution of the screen (which makes text harder to read), and the lack of compatibility among users' computers.

# The BENEFITS
*of working at* **ACME**

If this headline were bitmapped, it could be published in any medium, and displayed on any kind of computer, in precisely this format.

## The bitmap decision

Most computer programs store text as a series of codes that represent letters, fonts, and formatting. The words are "live," so they can be edited and searched (if the display software permits).

But when text is saved as a bitmapped image, the computer no longer recognizes the letters because they are now part of the image. The text can't be edited or searched.

The decision to bitmap text depends on other factors as well. Bitmapping freezes the format to ensure that it will be displayed correctly, but this substantially increases storage and memory requirements. Here's an example:

→ A screen with 400 words on it stored as text takes up only 4K.

→ The same screen stored as a color bitmap image takes up 300K.

### When text is stored as letters:

→ It takes up much less space.

→ It's easy to modify.

**But...**

→ Any visual attribute you give the text (font, size, formatting) has to be precisely reproduced by users' computers. This greatly reduces the freedom to design custom formats.

→ You may have to install fonts on users' computers and take other technically demanding steps to assure compatibility.

### When text is bitmapped:

→ It can have fancy styling and formatting.

→ You can always count on it looking right.

**But...**

→ It takes up a lot of room in memory and on disk.

→ The large sizes of the bitmap files affect performance as well as storage.

→ It's much more difficult to make revisions because words can't be selected or moved.

# Preserving the format

The way text looks on users' screens depends on factors that you cannot always control. For text to look the same way you designed it, the user's computer must have the right fonts, and the display software must produce the right format; this isn't always possible. But text can look exactly the way it was designed if it is bitmapped—turned into an image that permanently preserves its format.

Another way to preserve the format, if the product doesn't rely on specific multimedia playback software, is to convert it to portable document format (PDF) to preserve all the original text attributes. PDF is the file format that Adobe Acrobat produces from source documents created with various application tools. Just like bitmapped text, text in a PDF document is displayed with the correct fonts and formats regardless of the computer platform or available fonts. However, unlike a bitmap image, the text is "live," so users can electronically search, select, copy, and scale it to any size.

For products that aren't suitable for delivery as PDF documents, the bitmap decision is an important one, which has major consequences for the production process (see above).

## An alternative to scrolling fields

There's no question that scrolling fields for text are convenient. They're built into every authoring tool and can accommodate any amount of text. But scrolling fields do have drawbacks:

→ no custom formatting is possible inside a field

→ anti-aliasing isn't available at any size

→ built-in scrolling fields can spoil the look of an otherwise well-integrated screen design

Text that can't fit on a single screen doesn't have to be put into a scrolling field; it can be broken up into sections that are displayed on demand by the reader. When there's no scrolling field, the text can be designed to match the style of the screen, as can the buttons used to display text sections.

## Minimum sizes for text fonts

By definition, the things people do on computer have always been interactive. Computers and pe interact with words, numbers, and pictures. Wh different today is that interaction is ex things that used to be considered "pas activities—such as reading, watching simply being entertained. And t that the audience, not the creato controls the sequence, the pace.

By definition, the things people do on computer have always been interactive. Computers and pe interact with words, numbers, and pictures. Wh different today is that interaction is ex things that used to be considered "pas activities—such as reading, watchin; simply being entertained. And t that the audience, not the creato controls the sequence, the pace.

These examples show Bodoni Book type at 8-point, 10-point, and 12-point sizes, produced at printer resolution (left) and screen resolution (right). Although documents are frequently printed in 10-point type, text on the screen needs to be at least 12-point for most fonts to be comfortably readable.

Readability at different sizes should play a large role in choosing a screen font. As this example shows, a font that might be a good choice in print may have very poor letterforms on the screen at the required size.

## Anti-aliasing text

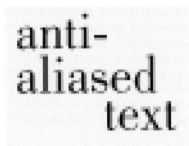

Anti-aliasing (discussed on p. 70) can soften edges so much as to make text hard to read. The examples here show 18-point text, enlarged to show detail. The finer of the two fonts has such thin strokes that they nearly disappear when the edges are softened by anti-aliasing. For such fine fonts, anti-aliasing should be used only on large display sizes. Bolder fonts with more uniform strokes can be anti-aliased at sizes down to 18-point if desired, but smaller sizes generally become too blurred.

## What's different about type on the screen?

| Text feature | Paper world | Screen world |
| --- | --- | --- |
| Size | High-resolution commercial typesetting systems produce crisp, easy-to-read type at all sizes. Eight-point and smaller text is common, with 9, 10, and 11-point the most common sizes for lengthy documents and books. | Twelve-point type is the smallest size that's comfortably readable in many fonts, with others starting even higher. |
| Readability | Fonts with curved serifs, such as Times, are often said to be the most readable, but any good text font is relatively easy to read. | All fonts work at large sizes, but at smaller sizes fonts should have serifs and strokes of even thickness for best legibility. (There are also ergonomic issues, including eye fatigue, associated with reading on computer screens.) |
| Letter spacing | Extra-tight spacing is often desirable in display type, and it can be controlled to within hundredths of an inch. | Tight spacing works on very large type, but anti-aliasing causes edges to bleed together. Spacing is more difficult to control. |
| Leading (space between lines of type) | No restrictions. | Leading should be two or more points higher than font size for comfortable reading on the screen. Tight leading in some fonts can cause the bottoms of letters to be cut off. |
| Line length | Since long unbroken lines are more difficult to read, short columns are recommended, in widths that vary according to type size. | Same basic rules apply, but since the minimum type size on the screen is larger, column width is less of a factor. |
| Color and contrast | No color restrictions, but higher contrast means better readability. | The softening effect of anti-aliasing reduces the contrast of letter edges, making extremes of contrast necessary so readers can make out text against background art. |
| Amount of text on page or screen | Not an issue. | Because the screen has much lower resolution than a page, a screen that's filled with text can be much harder to read. |

## The screen on the screen

What should be in the video window when no video is playing? The first frame is often used as a placeholder, but in this case there are several segments that might be played. The designer of this product came up with a unique solution that highlights a part of the background photo to give the sense of a video "window."

When the user selects a video segment, it begins to play in the highlighted region of the screen. Users can stop or restart the segment by clicking the video window, or start a new segment by clicking one of the buttons at left.

## Good reasons to use video

→ A personal message needs to be communicated by a specific individual.

→ You need to show something in live action, such as an artistic performance or an instructional role-playing scenario.

→ You need to demonstrate something functional, such as a tool or a vehicle.

→ You need to show an object or a place from several different points of view or in some other way that a single image couldn't accomplish.

→ You want to teach something that would be expensive or impractical for viewers to experience in a lab or other real-world setting.

→ You're using video as art.

# Video

**Video has an astonishing power to bring life to the computer screen. An image that just sits there is no match for one that talks and moves. But the novelty wears off almost immediately if the video doesn't present a compelling message or experience.**

Video production is a highly evolved art and technology. It's a world of sophisticated equipment, studio facilities, and professional skills that are quite different from other aspects of creating interactive products.

The great illusion of desktop video is that the availability of desktop tools makes it easy for everyone with a computer and a video camera to create quality video productions.

The best digital video starts with the best analog video: a professional director and actors; a crew for camera, lighting, and sound; and post-production specialists to do the editing and digitizing.

Few project budgets can support a professional video crew from start to finish, but any step of the process that can be done by a professional will improve the overall results.

## Digital video decisions

→ **How large should the video window be?**

The size of the video is a design decision, but it's also a technical decision: the larger the video, the more space it takes up on disk and the more processing power it requires to run smoothly. You can design the video on the screen only after you've determined what size can play with reliable quality on users' computers.

→ **How long should the video play?**

Long video segments take up a lot of disk space (10 megabytes per minute or more is common), and take a long time to download (if users are downloading them). More important, though, is the tolerance of the audience. What are they willing to sit through? Longer segments need more variety and attention to pacing. Thirty seconds of a talking head can seem like forever, while a minute-long action sequence may seem short in comparison.

## Custom—shaped video images

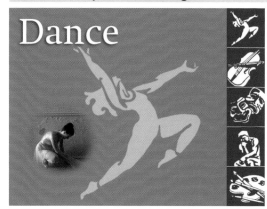

A video window can be any shape that suits the interface. This round video window is a good match for the soft, fluid lines of this interface.

This irregular window supports the rough, hand-hewn look of the screen.

The digital video image itself is always straight-edged. The apparent shape of the video window is produced by composing a mask of the background into the video clip so that it appears in every frame.

---

An interactive product may contain video from many sources, and the style and content of each segment may or may not match other elements in the interface. Integrating these diverse styles is where desktop video software can really shine, by making it possible to creatively alter colors, shapes, and other attributes of both the video image and the video window.

Many techniques can help to visually integrate video on the screen:

→ Customize the shape of the video window to make it blend into the background.

→ Design the background to look like an extension of the visuals in the video.

→ Create custom video controls to match the interface style, rather than using the built-in video controller bar.

Playing video makes great demands on a computer's memory, storage space, and speed. Add to this that the video image in most interactive products delivers lower quality than users are accustomed to on their home TV screens, at a tiny fraction of the size, and it's clear that the subject matter had better be interesting, relevant to the content, and fun to watch.

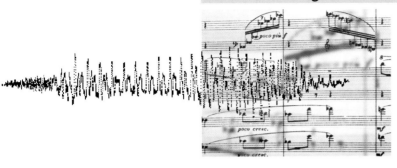

## When sound is digital

The key characteristic of digital sound is its sampling rate, or the resolution at which the sound is digitized. The higher the sampling rate, the better the resulting sound quality. However, as usual, there is a tradeoff between quality and performance: high-resolution sound files are extremely large (over one megabyte per minute for acceptable quality; several times that for audio CD quality), so the memory and processing power needed to play them can degrade overall product performance.

A great benefit of digital sound is that it's easy to edit and modify. Audio processing software displays sound graphically so that any portion can be selected, cut, and pasted almost as easily as words in a document. These sound tools provide extensive options for modifying sound attributes such as loudness or tempo, and producing special effects such as smooth fades and dissolves.

# Sound

**Some designers believe that sound accounts for more than half of the experience of using an interactive product. Whether or not this is true, it's certain that *bad* sound can ruin the entire experience.**

Some interfaces contain no sound at all, either due to limitations in space or speed, or because they're designed as strictly visual experiences. Others feature audio clips that users can download, but since these aren't integrated into the experience, they play no direct role in the interface. However, when music, sound effects, and narration are integrated into the interface, they can play a significant role in both the design and the content.

Creating the audio portion of an interactive product is called sound design. Professional sound designers provide services that can include locating and selecting music and narration talent, producing and directing the audio recording sessions, and converting audio media into high-quality computer sound files. As with digital video, the key to good digital sound is starting with an audio source of the best possible quality.

## Sources of sound

Musical styling would be easy if it were possible to browse record stores for CDs that match the mood, style, and subject of your product. But since commercial recordings are usually too expensive to license, the alternatives are clip media sources for pre-recorded sound, and professional studios for original soundtracks.

→ Clip media sources have libraries of every imaginable sound effect and music style, available on audio CDs and as digital files (see the Resource Guide).

→ Professional studios and musicians can be a surprisingly affordable step beyond clip media. A small music studio may be a reasonable one-stop source for composition, performance, recording, and digitizing.

If the project calls for a narrator, choosing the right one is critical. When the speaker's face and gestures aren't there to personalize his or her voice, listeners notice every flaw in diction or phrasing. This doesn't mean that narration should be avoided. But it does suggest that professional voice talent is a must, and that the talent should be carefully screened for style. Even a highly experienced announcer might be the wrong choice for a training course on people skills, if his prior experience was on a TV game show.

Composers, musicians, audio specialists, and voice talent can be located through specialized industry directories (a few are listed in the Resource Guide).

# Sound strategies

Successfully integrating sound into an interface requires special attention to mixing and timing. The volume levels of music, narration, and sound effects must be balanced at every moment to produce the correct emphasis and mood. This isn't just a concern for entertainment products, but for every type of communication. Although synchronizing sounds to changes on the screen can be technically demanding, it can add substantial impact to the presentation.

An economical strategy for sound design can be to choose one long, multi-part musical piece as the project's score. Using different portions of this music to accompany different parts of the content can produce a family of musical segments with both diversity and continuity. This strategy will also save you many hours of time screening multiple, unrelated sources for suitable clips.

Sound is the ultimate editorial tool. It can make or break the tone of an interactive product, and have a tremendous influence on users' perceptions of the content. (Think of a visual introduction to a training course accompanied by heavy metal rock music, or by a quiet, meditative flute solo.) Just as the wrong music, sound effect, or narrator works against your message, the effort invested in choosing the right sounds results in more focused and effective communication.

## Animating in the authoring tool

True animation, where objects and characters move and change in every frame, is usually stored and played as video, so integrating it into an interface is like working with digital video. However, there's also a range of techniques that can animate interface elements as they are assembled in the authoring tool.

### Elements that change
Simple animation can be done in the authoring tool by rapidly displaying a sequence of images.

### Elements that move
Words and images can be moved around the screen to entertain viewers, emphasize content, or support narration (as shown here).

### Elements that appear/disappear
The screen can be animated by introducing different elements over time, as in this preview of topics.

### Screen transitions
The most common form of motion on the screen, transitions can be the simplest way to enliven the visual presentation.

# Animating the screen

**There are many ways to animate an interface. If your budget permits, these can include full-screen computerized animation and frame-by-frame cartoon drawings. On a more modest scale, animating the screen can simply mean giving life and motion to the media elements you already have.**

Motion on the screen can help accomplish several presentation goals:

→ Establish a sequence: Bringing items into view one at a time helps to introduce topics and suggest a viewing order.

→ Create emphasis: Items that move or change shape can call attention to a topic or prompt users to take an action.

→ Create a visual bridge: Transitions move users gracefully between topics.

A good animator can create nearly anything you can imagine; the limitation on what you can design is more likely to be performance than production. For example, an effect such as zooming into a part of the screen requires many full-screen images to be quickly loaded from a disk and displayed—something beyond the processing power of most users' computers. Like video, animation can quickly push your product beyond the capabilities of users' equipment.

Animating words doesn't have to mean flashing bullet items on the screen one at a time, a popular approach in many slide-show-type products. Another approach is shown here. The title first appears in the center, and then moves to the top to make way for the content that users interact with.

A transition doesn't have to be an immediate change. In this introductory sequence, the appearance of each image is synchronized to its introduction in the narration, using the sequence of topics to tell a story. The images fade onto the screen at the appropriate moment using an individual transition for each.

# Transitions

A transition is a special effect that provides a visual bridge when images change on the screen. Film and TV transitions are part of the popular media vocabulary: all viewers know, consciously or not, that certain transitions have a certain significance (for example, a fade to black means that a scene has ended). So using a particular transition in an interactive product is more than just an aesthetic choice; it also implies meaning.

In the world of video, most transitions affect the whole screen because each video frame is a single unit. On the computer, however, there's no need for a transition to affect the whole screen. Objects can be brought on or off independently of each other in whatever way best suits the design.

Transitions can play an important role in the look and feel of an interface, but they need to be used with restraint.

Many authoring tools offer an extensive library of built-in transitions, from checkerboards to venetian blinds. If these are overused or applied at the wrong times, the effect can be jarring or gimmicky. A plain fade or dissolve can be used in nearly any situation and repeated often, but a diagonal wipe used over and over can quickly become annoying. Most of the time, transitions work best when they are subtle and unobtrusive.

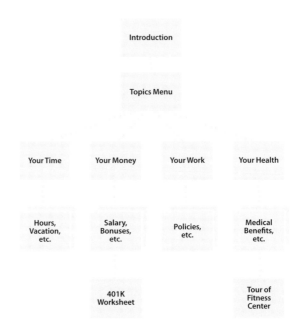

# Putting it all together

**At some point in the process—it doesn't matter when—you begin to integrate the pieces of the interface into a prototype. The prototype is the final step of presentation design, but integration can begin at any time.**

Integration means bringing all the interface elements together, using the authoring tool, to create a functional framework or shell for the product. As the content is developed and the design elements are integrated, the shell progressively replaces the conceptual framework represented by the flowchart and storyboard.

The sooner integration into the authoring tool begins, the sooner it becomes possible to solve the inevitable problems that arise when pieces of the project are brought together. At first, the shell can simply be a place to store elements as they are completed, and needn't be highly interactive. It's helpful just to see everything come together in a way that indicates how the real screens will look and behave.

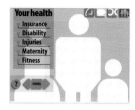

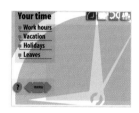
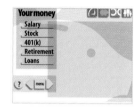

Building the shell means using the authoring tool to mock up each frame in the storyboard:

→ creating a place in the shell to represent each screen

→ importing the content, graphics, and media

→ adding the navigation links to and from each screen

→ creating at least some of the interaction controls, if resources permit

As the elements are integrated and the prototype screens take shape, it becomes evident whether the flowchart, storyboard, and presentation design work as intended. Where do they break down? How should the breaks be repaired? This is the time to fix links that lead nowhere, confusing directions, ambiguous choices, and anything else that couldn't be spotted on paper.

The integration process is also where give-and-take occurs between design and engineering, as it becomes clear that some design features are too hard to implement, or cause product performance to degrade. Here's where the designer's knowledge about digital media can make a significant difference in avoiding and solving problems.

In every design decision, choosing simplicity will pay you back in ease of production, better performance, and ease of use.

# The prototype

**A prototype is a preliminary, incomplete, on-screen version of the product. It does not need commercial-quality refinement; the degrees of detail and interaction built into it can be scaled to fit your resources. How far it makes sense to take the prototype depends on how it will be used.**

The scenarios on the facing page describe three possible next steps. The project may not have formal approval yet, in which case the next step would be to get it approved. The project may be ready to try out on real people, so the next step would be getting it ready for user testing. Or the project may be ready to go into production, in which case its expenses are about to rise dramatically, requiring more long-range preparations.

No matter what the next steps are, be prepared for the likelihood that almost every aspect of the project will continue to change and evolve.

Your project goals are your compass; don't lose sight of them. In every design decision, choosing simplicity will pay you back in ease of production, better performance, and ease of use.

# What's next?

## Sell the idea

If the project hasn't been formally approved yet, you may have had little or nothing to spend so far, on a prototype or anything else.

The goal in this case is to create just enough material so you have (and can convey convincingly) a good sense of what would be required—in time, money, and people—to do the job well.

If the goal is selling, the prototype might include:

→ a detailed description of the project, including your best efforts at a flowchart and content inventory list

→ a proposed budget and schedule

→ if you have the resources to create it, a paper storyboard that outlines the planned interactivity

→ again, if you have the resources, a set of design sketches or screens that show possible directions for the visual design

## Test the design

Audience research becomes user testing when you can stop asking people what they think about an idea and let them try the real thing.

To get the most out of a usability test, it's more useful to have one complete section of the project working well than to have bits and pieces of the entire thing. The goal is not to walk the test subjects through the prototype (that's a demo, not a test), but to turn them loose with it and see what they do: what they manage easily, where they get confused, what they try that doesn't work, where they simply give up.

If the goal is testing, the prototype might include:

→ a main menu that shows all major topic areas (even the non-functional ones)

→ for each functional topic, a fully implemented path all the way through to the most detailed level of content

→ worst-case screens (that is, those likely to cause users the most difficulty), so you can ask for comments on possible solutions

→ alternate designs, so you can ask which one people prefer

## Build the product

A pre-production prototype needs to describe the product well enough that people on the project team can use it to get to work. All basic decisions about content, organization, navigation, interaction, and design have to be spelled out in the prototype so they're available to everyone on the team.

If the goal is building, the prototype might include:

→ all project management documents including a schedule, budget, and tracking chart that shows major deadlines and interdependencies (for example, video digitizing can't begin until video is shot)

→ descriptive documents including the complete flowchart, detailed paper storyboard, and design sketches or screens

→ an incomplete but fully functional interactive prototype, created in the authoring tool, that takes the detailed storyboard to the desired level of production quality

# interactivity =
## *communication + choice*

In the end, interactivity is people using new media to communicate ideas, knowledge, and art in much the same way that people have always communicated. The core of good interactive communication is still a strong message and a clear presentation. The design process still calls for research, creativity, and skillful execution. The one new variable in the equation is the element of audience choice. And choice can take users in unpredictable directions and combine elements of the design in unpredictable ways. That's why interactivity calls for a greater commitment to planning, to usability, and to making the pieces work together than communication has ever demanded before.

# Resource Guide

Designing for the computer screen calls for all kinds of images, sounds, and other media elements to help you tell your story. There are many sources for these elements, and new ones appear daily. A few are listed on these pages.

## Clip media providers

Clip media providers sell images, music, sound effects, and video clips for which all usage rights have been cleared. For a one-time fee, these companies provide fully digitized materials that are ready to use on a computer. Most clip media collections are organized and sold by topic, so you might buy a CD-ROM filled with 50 nature scenes or 100 drumrolls, rather than just one item.

Once you've purchased clip media, you can use it as many times as you like and in any way that you like. However, if you use the materials in products intended for commercial sale or broadcast, the providers typically charge additional fees.

## Stock agencies

Stock agencies have collections of high-quality images, music, and video. Unlike clip media, stock items must be selected or requested individually from the agency's collection and licensed for a single use. The agency's fee depends not only on which items you choose, but on how widely the product containing those items will be distributed.

Stock media are substantially more expensive than clip media, but they fill a different type of need. You can call a stock agency with specific requests for a type of image, and they will research and fill the order, often sending you a number of candidates to choose from.

## Media services

Media services are experienced in locating and licensing content materials quickly and economically. Although it's possible to do this work yourself, hiring a media service is highly recommended if

→ you have no prior experience obtaining permissions or negotiating licensing fees

→ you need to obtain a large number of items

→ you are trying to get the rights to use original works (a portrait in a museum, a video clip from the evening news, a song from your favorite vocal group) from their creator, owner, or publisher

## Media directories

Producing original images, sounds, or video is a part of most interactive projects, and it requires finding professionals with the right skills. The search can begin with personal references from people you trust, or by seeking out the creators of past work that you've seen and liked. To make the search easier, directories and sourcebooks are available that list professionals for every aspect of media production. For illustration and photography, these directories include samples from hundreds of artists in every imaginable style.

# Clip media providers

**Corel**
613-728-3733
Thousands of images, photos, symbols, and fonts.

**Digital Stock**
800-545-4514
Photos. Emphasis on scenics/nature, but many other subjects covered as well. Catalog disc available.

**Image Club**
800-661-9410
Extensive collections of typefaces, clip art, and photos, including the Object Gear collection.

**Janus Professional Sound Library**
800-526-8739
Music and sound effects.

**Killer Tracks**
800-877-0078
Music and sound effects.

**Macromedia**
415-442-0200
Images, video, music, sound effects, and animation.

**PhotoDisc, Inc.**
800-528-3472
**http://www.photodisc.com**
Over 8000 images. Features special collections for business, nature, travel, and many more subjects. Catalog disc available.

**Sound Ideas**
800-387-3030 (US)
800-665-3000 (Canada)
Enormous sound-effects collection.

**Ultimate Symbol**
800-870-7940
A collection of clip art images—ornaments, geometrics, and all types of standard symbols and icons.

# Stock agencies

**Archive Photos / Archive New Media**
800-886-3980
An international photo and video collection featuring people and events in current and past history.

**The Bettmann Archive**
212-777-6200
Over 16 million images. Though best known for their historical and political collections, they have everything.

**Comstock**
800-225-2727
Over 4 million photos. Now offers CD-ROM and on-line downloading.

**The Image Bank**
800-842-4624
A vast collection of high-quality photos for professional uses of all types. Catalogs and PhotoCD browser available.

**Nonstock**
212-633-2388
Unusual photos and illustrations for out-of-the-ordinary projects.

**Seymour**
800-764-7427
An on-line image service that provides access to over 250,000 images from over 30 stock sources. You can search, price, order, and download without getting out of your chair.

**Worldwide Television News**
800-526-1161
Extensive news footage of US and international events.

**WPA Film Library**
800-777-2223
Over 15,000 hours of historical and stock video footage.

# Media services

**Access Research Partners**
800-593-3463
Photo, video, and music research; copyright and trademark searches; and more.

**Art Resource**
212-505-8700
Specializes in locating images from museum collections worldwide.

**BZ/Rights and Permissions, Inc.**
212-580-0615
A rights clearance service for all types of materials: music, literature, photos, film and TV clips, art.

**Photo Productions**
**415-664-6600**
For all still photography needs. Photo research, photo licensing, photo permissions, and management/coordination of photo shoots.

**Total Clearance**
**415-389-1531**
Clearance of rights to film and video properties for reuse in new media projects.

## Media directories

**American Showcase Illustration**
**212-764-7300**
Contains work samples from hundreds of artists. Good for style ideas as well as art candidates. Companion directory of photographers also available.

**The Reel Directory**
**707-584-8083**
A film, video, multi-image, multi-media resource directory. Contains listings for everything from actors and audio producers to underwater photography and video walls. US West Coast emphasis.

**The Workbook Directories**
**800-547-2688**
A comprehensive series of directories listing artists, photographers, stock agencies, production services—and even a directory of directories.

## Training resources

**Ignition**
**415-221-4385**
Ignition is the information design studio founded by the authors of this book. In addition to design consulting, Ignition provides seminars and customized courses on how to communicate with new media.

# Credits

**Editor-in-Chief**
Patrick Ames / Adobe Press

**Book design**
MetaDesign, San Francisco / Jeff Zwerner, with
Joshua Distler and David Nong

**Cover Design**
Jeff Zwerner / MetaDesign, San Francisco

**Cover Photography**
Kevin Ng

**Art direction**
Illustrations:
Ray Kristof and Amy Satran / Ignition,
San Francisco
Part openers and photography:
Jeff Zwerner / MetaDesign, San Francisco

**Production**
Maureen Hands / MetaDesign, San Francisco

**Pre-press**
MetaGraphics, PaloAlto

**Printing**
Shepard Poorman, Indianapolis

**Reviewers**
Eli Cochran, Ethan Diamond, Maureen Hands,
Terry Irwin, George Jardine, Patricia Kellison,
Michael Nolan, Laura Perry, Deborah Robbins,
David Rogelberg, Neal Satran, Jeff Zwerner

**Special thanks**
To Katy Beierle and PhotoDisc Inc., for
generously making their digital photo library
available for use in this book.

And to Deborah Gale, Ann Gingras, Debra
Goldentyer, Joanne Maass, Mark Schaeffer

**Illustration and photo credits**
mouse maze facing page 1, 16, 52, 90
Patrick Merrell, New York

Page 14
Black Anvil is ™ and © 1995 Top Cow
Productions; artwork is © 1995 Top Cow
Productions

Page 19
© 1995, The Voyager Company, New York, NY
View the current Voyager site at
http://www.voyagerco.com

Page 22
© 1941 Turner Entertainment Co.
All rights reserved

Page 27
Photograph obtained from an unknown source
and printed in the frontispiece of *Ockham on
Aristotle's Physics*
Courtesy of The Franciscan Institute,
St. Bonaventure University

Page 28, 38, 40 left, 41 center and right, 42, 44, 45, 49, 50 left and right, 51 right, 69, 73, 75, 82, 83 top left and right, 84 top center and right, 85, 86 far left, 91 top left and bottom left, 93 left, 97, 99, 105 left and center, 108, 111 left, 112, 114 bottom, 117 top right
Courtesy of PhotoDisc, Inc.

Page 28 Great Wall photo
© China News Digest

Page 35
Courtesy of Mackerel, Toronto, Canada
Mackerel's response to being poked in the eye!

Page 39 left
Courtesy of Clement Mok designs
Designed by Claire Barry,
Associate Creative Director

Page 39 right
© Sumeria 1993

Page 40 right, 55
© Adobe Systems, Inc.

Page 46, 71, 87 right, 97 bottom, 101 top left, 111 right, 114 third from top, 115
© Amnesty International USA
(From *Amnesty Interactive,* created by Ignition, illustrated by Nancy Nimoy)

Page 63
Courtesy of Archive Photos

Page 68
Courtesy of Image Club/Object Gear

Page 71 top, 101 top left
Photos for Amnesty International created by Robin Raj/dawg and Doyle Advertising
Photo p. 71 by Matt Mahurin
Photo p. 101 by Eric Meola

Page 80
Jim Theodore, Illustrated Alaskan Moose Studio, 5 West Main Street, Westerville, OH 43081

Page 82, 101 bottom right, 106, 114 top
Courtesy of Scholastic, Inc., Palo Alto
(Designed by Ignition, illustrated by Patrick Merrell)

Page 83 bottom, 89
Illustrations by Oenone Terril, San Francisco

Page 84 left, 85
*100 + 1 Years of Hungarian Posters,* The History of Hungarian Poster Design 1885–1986

Page 87, 96, 101 bottom left, 110
Courtesy of PWS Publishing Co., Boston, MA
(From *VizAbility,* designed by MetaDesign)

Page 88
"Gelb-Rot-Blau" 1925, Vasily Kandinsky
Photo by Philippe Migeat
© Centre G. Pompidou

Page 101 top right
Courtesy of Apple Computer, Inc.

Page 103 top right, 104
Nancy Nimoy, Los Angeles

All other illustrations
Conceived by Ignition, produced by MetaDesign

# Index

**A**

access 27, 32, 43–47
  direct 44
  levels of 46
  random 47
  routes 32, 33, 42, 43, 44, 47
  types of 45
Adobe Acrobat 40, 57, 107
animation 20, 25, 95, 114–115
anti-aliasing 69, 70–71, 79, 108, 109
assumptions
  users' 48
  yours 11–13, 52
audience 1, 8–9, 26, 35, 40, 41, 111
  defining 11, 14–15
  research 16–17, 119
audio. see sound
authoring tools 9, 18, 66, 106
  built-in features of 74, 108, 114, 115
  prototyping with 116, 117, 119
  types of 20–21

**B**

backgrounds 70, 71, 89, 95, 96–97, 110, 111
behavior
  of people 50–51, 91
  of products 48, 50–51, 53, 67

bitmapping 106, 107
breaking the rules 102
bringing instead of sending 46
browsers 18, 19, 21, 51
budget projection 25, 119
buttons. see controls

**C**

CD-ROM 4, 9, 18, 19, 20, 23, 47, 59, 76, 77, 78
clip media 113, 122
color 67, 72–75, 109
color depth 72, 74, 77, 79
color palettes 67, 72–75
compatibility 66, 67, 106, 107
compression 67, 76–77
  software for 77
computers. see equipment
consensus 25
consistency 53, 92, 102
construction kit 94
content categories 28–29, 30, 32
content inventory list 22–23, 119
content you don't own 25, 113, 122
continuous-tone images 69
control, by users. see interaction, control of

controls 36, 49, 52, 53, 88, 95, 110, 116
  as integral design elements 101
  built-in vs. custom 56–57, 108–109
  designing 42, 43, 51, 55, 100–103, 108, 111
  functions of 54, 100
  highlighting 50, 51
  positioning 50, 100, 102
critical tasks
  information design 8
  interaction design 36
  presentation design 64

**D**

data rate 77
delivery media and methods 9, 15, 18–19, 23, 66
dependencies 53, 119
designer 1, 35, 47, 48, 76, 85, 103, 117
design
  decisions 12, 29, 31, 53, 66, 77, 78, 85, 93, 100, 106, 111, 113, 115, 117, 118
  plan 8–9
  variables 15
desktop video software 77, 110, 111
digital media 65, 66–79, 117
  conversion to 23, 67, 77, 79, 110, 112
disk space 67, 107, 111, 112
dithering 75
DPI (dots per inch) 69
documents, interactive 4, 18, 21, 25, 37, 46, 59

**E**

ease of use 49, 118
electronic document software 21
engineering 20–21, 65, 76, 117
environment 14–15
equipment
    users' 15, 65, 67, 72, 74, 78, 79, 106, 107, 111, 114
    yours 66, 79
ergonomic issues 109
examples of products. see product examples
expectations, users' 48, 111
eye fatigue 109

**F**

feedback 50
floppy disk 25
flowchart 5, 30, 32–33, 36, 42, 43, 44, 58, 116, 117, 119
fonts 107, 108, 109
frame rate 77
frames 77, 110, 111, 114, 115
frames per second 77
functionality 52–57
    macro view 53
    micro view 54–55, 56–57

**G, H**

goals 8–9, 10–13, 17, 37, 118
grids 92–93
guidance 36, 38–39
hierarchy 30, 32–33, 42, 86
home page 40, 42, 78, 84–85
housekeeping chores 42
HTML (Hypertext Markup Language) 21
hyperlinks 57

**I, J, K**

icons 89, 103
image maps 40–41, 89
image-processing tools 74, 75, 77, 105, 106
images 20–21, 95. see also bitmapping.
    component 104
    cropping 105
    integration of 105
    processing 79, 105
    shadowing 105
    sources of 84, 122–125
    standalone 104
    styles 84–85, 104
    transitions between 115
    vignetting 105
information design 5, 7–9, 32, 36, 64
    building blocks of 8
    critical tasks of 8
information structures 27, 30–31, 32

integration of elements 96–97, 98–99, 101, 105, 110, 111, 113, 116–117
interaction design 5, 35–37, 52, 64
    critical tasks of 36
interactive documents 4, 18, 21, 25, 37, 46, 59
interaction
    control of 19, 35, 37, 53, 56–57, 110
    defined 1
    forms of 37, 42
interactivity. see interaction
interface
    design 3, 64, 88
    elements of 94–95
    families 86–87
    style 81
Internet 4, 9, 21, 78

**L**

layout 88–93
    conventions for 90–91
leading (of type) 109
learning curve 20
legibility. see readability
letter spacing 109
licensing. see media licensing
links. see access routes, hyperlinks

## M, N, O

main menu 30, 31, 33, 40, 42, 43, 119
media licensing 113, 122
medium of delivery 9, 15, 18–19, 23, 66
memory 67, 107, 111, 112
metaphors 40–41, 57
   functional 41
   navigational 41
modes 54
mood 113
multimedia authoring tools 20
multimedia programs 41, 59
music 24, 112, 113
narration 112, 113
navigation 19, 21, 32, 42–47, 50, 117
net surfing 47
networks
   private 18–19, 67
   public 18–19, 67, 78

## P

PDF (portable document format) 107
paging vs. scrolling 57
palettes. see color palettes
panels 95, 98–99

paper clip example 71
performance 65, 67, 76–77, 78, 107, 111, 112, 114, 117, 118
pixels 68, 72, 73, 75
planning tools 25
point of view 31, 45
portable document format (PDF) 107
presentation design 5, 63–64, 116, 117
   critical tasks of 64
presentation software 21
print media 38, 108, 109
problems and solutions
   animation 114
   anti-aliasing 71
   backgrounds 97
   dithering 75
   functionality 54–55
   layout 89
   panels 99
   stylistic unity 84–85, 86–87
   transitions 115
   video windows 110, 111
process chart 5, 11
process overview 4–5
product definition 10–13

product examples
   arts catalog 83, 89
   bicycle club home page 84–85
   interactive company brochure 22–23, 24, 31
   interactive employee benefits guide 29–30, 59, 61, 83, 86, 93, 97, 99, 102, 116–117
product usage 15
project planning 22–25
prototype 5, 64, 65, 116–119
public media 18–19
public network 18–19

## Q, R

quality tradeoffs 77, 78, 107, 111, 112, 114
quitting 51
readability 108, 109
red flag list 25
redundancy 49
registration 93
resolution 67, 68–69, 79, 106, 108, 109

## S

sales demo 14
sample products. see product examples
sampling rate 112
screen resolution. see resolution
scripting 20
scrolling vs. paging 57, 108
searching text 57, 107
shell 116–117
shortcuts 51
simplicity 32, 49, 100, 118
sound 20–21, 95, 112–113
    controlling 56
    design 112, 113
    effects 112, 113
    integration of 113
    processing software 112
    production 79, 112, 113
    sources of 112, 113, 122–125
storyboard 4, 5, 36, 52, 58–61, 63, 64, 116, 117, 119
style 64, 80–87, 105, 111, 113
Survival Kit 66–79
synchronization 20, 21, 113

## T

task projection 25
text 20–21, 95, 106–109
    amount on page or screen 109
    animating 115
    bitmapping 107
    color of 109
    controlling 57
    editing 107
    fonts 107, 108, 109
    leading of 109
    letter spacing of 109
    line length of 109
    readability of 108, 109
    scrolling fields for 108
    searching 57, 107
    size of 108, 109
themes 82–83
time 59
traditional media 38, 90, 92, 108, 109, 115
transitions 20, 21, 114, 115
travel 44, 46
trouble signs 25
type. see fonts; text
typography 106, 108–109

## U, V

usability 27, 32, 48–51
    guidelines for 49–51
    key principles of 48–49
users. see audience
user testing 119
video 20–21, 23, 76–77, 95, 110–111, 114, 115
    controlling 56
    integration of 110, 111
    length of 111
    processing software 110, 111
    production 79, 110
    size of 111
    sources of 122–125
    windows 110, 111
vignetting. see images, vignetting
voice talent. see narration

## W, X, Y, Z

what this book is about 4
who this book is for 3
windows 95, 98–99, 110, 111
World Wide Web 18, 21, 23, 39
worst case 55, 119